LIST OF SNAKES IN THE INDIAN MUSEUM

LIST

OF

SNAKES

IN THE

INDIAN MUSEUM.

W. L. SCLATER, M. A., F. Z. S.

GYAN

Published by

GYAN

Gyan Publishing House
5, Ansari Road
Daryaganj, New Delhi-110002
Phone: 011-47034999, 9811692060
E-mail: books@gyanbooks.com

Distribution Network
gyanbooks.com
India, USA, Canada, UK, Australia, France

ISBN: 978-81-212-8490-5 (PB)
First Published, 1891

2nd Impression 2023

Printed at: Gyan Press, Delhi.

LIST OF SNAKES IN THE INDIAN MUSEUM
Author: W. L. SCLATER

LIST

OF

SNAKES

IN THE

INDIAN MUSEUM.

BY

W. L. SCLATER, M. A., F. Z. S.,

DEPUTY SUPERINTENDENT OF THE INDIAN MUSEUM.

CALCUTTA:

PRINTED BY ORDER OF THE TRUSTEES OF THE INDIAN MUSEUM.

1891.

INTRODUCTION.

The following is a mere List of the Snakes in the Indian Museum; it has not seemed necessary to give descriptions or the synonymy of the various species, this having in the case of the Indian forms been quite recently, thoroughly done by Mr. Boulenger in his Reptiles of British India; and in the case of the exotic forms neither are our collections large enough, nor is my knowledge sufficiently extensive for the task.

I have therefore contented myself with giving in each case the Author of the specific name and a reference to the best description, not necessarily the original one, to which I have been able to get access.

The following table shows the number of the species and specimens of Indian and Exotic Snakes in the Museum:

	NUMBERS.	
	of species.	of specimens.
Indian ...	210	2615
Exotic ...	140	386
Total ...	350	3001

The number of Snakes described by Mr. Boulenger in his recent work on the Reptiles of the Indian Empire and Ceylon amounts in all to 264, to which number from an examination of the Snakes in the Indian Museum I have been able to add thirteen, of which five are new and eight are exotic species not mentioned in Mr. Boulenger's work,* and one species, Dipsas multifasciatus, which had formerly been confused with Dipsas ceylonensis has been discriminated.

This raises the number of Snakes in the Indian Empire to 278; of these, as will be seen from above, the Museum possesses examples of 210 so that there are still 68 deficiencies wanting to make the collection of the Museum quite complete.

Many of these 68 species of which a list will be found below are unique or very rare, and it will probably be

* The following are the thirteen snakes added to the Indian Fauna: Ablabes stoliczkae, Simotes purpurascens, Simotes woodmasoni, Zaoccys tenasserimensis, Tropidonotus vibakari, Tropidonotus pealii, Tropidonotus nicobarensis, Tropidonotus triangnligerus, Dipsas cynodon, Dipsas fusca, Megaerophis flaviceps, Amblycephalus carinatus and Amblycephalus moellendorffi.

long before the Museum collection can be rendered quite complete.

The number of type specimens in the Museum amounts in all to 30, of which 12 were described by Blyth, 5 by Blanford and myself respectively, 3 by Stoliczka and Anderson and 2 by Theobald. A complete list of the types also will be found below.

The classification adopted in the following list is that of Mr. Boulenger's in his Reptiles of British India; this classification however includes only those genera found within the limits of the Indian Empire, but I have endeavoured, as far as possible, to interpolate the exotic genera into their rightful positions.

In this, however, I fear, I may have made a good many errors, still there is absolutely no modern standard work on Snakes, and I thought it better to try and adopt a new classification than to fall back on obsolete arrangements.

With regard to nomenclature I have of course followed Boulenger throughout for Indian Snakes; for North American Snakes I have made use of a monograph by Mr. Garman published in the 8th volume of the Memoirs of the Museum of the Comparative Zoology at Harvard College, Cambridge, Mass., for the Australian Snakes I have used Krefft's Snakes of Australia and for European forms Schreiber's Herpetologia Europaea; for African and South American forms I have been unable to find any more modern general work than Günther's Catalogue of Colubrine Snakes in the British Museum, and Gray's previous Catalogue of the non-colubrine forms.

The principal donors of the snakes in the Indian Museum are as follows:—

Col. Godwin Austen, Mr. S. E. Peal and Capt. J. Butler from Assam; Col. Beddome from the South India, Mr. Blanford from Persia and also from many other parts of India; Mr. J. Gammie from Sikkim, other donors from various parts of India are Dr. Anderson, Mr. W. Theobald, Dr. F. Stoliczka and Sir J. Fayrer.

Description of the new species and notes on the Geographical distribution and other points of interest, made out during the examination of the Indian Museum collection, will be found in a paper in the 60th volume of the Journal of the Asiatic Society which is referred to throughout in the List.

In conclusion I have to thank Mr. Boulenger of the British Museum for help in naming several of the most interesting forms and for many hints and suggestions.

LIST OF TYPE SPECIMENS IN THE INDIAN MUSEUM

WITH REFERENCES TO THE ORIGINAL DESCRIPTIONS.

Typhlops theobaldianus, Stoliczka, J. A. S. B. xl, 1871, p. 429.
Typhlops persicus, Blanford, Ann. Mag. N. H. (4) xiv, p. 34.
Calamaria stahlknechti, Stoliczka, J. A. S. B. xlii, 1873, p. 119.
Trachischium fuscum (*Calamaria*), Blyth, J. A. S. B. xxiii, 1854, p. 288.
Trachischium tenuiceps (*Calamaria*), Blyth, J. A. S. B. xxiii, 1854, p. 288.
Blythia reticulata (*Calamaria*), Blyth, J. A. S. B. xxiii, 1854, p. 287.
Lycodon gammiei (*Ophites*); Blanford, J. A. S. B. xlvii, 1878, p. 130.
Hydrophobus davisonii (*Ulupe*), Blanford, J. A. S. B. xlvii, 1878, p. 129.
Pseudocyclophis bicolor (*Calamaria*), Blyth, J. A. S. B. xxiii, 1854, p. 289.
Pseudocyclophis persicus (*Cyclophis*), Anderson, P. Z. S., 1872, p. 392.
Ablabes scriptus, Theobald, Journ. Linn. Soc., x, 1868, p. 42.
Ablabes stoliczkae, Sclater, J. A. S. B. lx, 1891, p. 234.
Ablabes nicobariensis, Stoliczka, J. A. S. B. xxxix, 1870, p. 184.
Simotes woodmasoni, Sclater, J. A. S. B. lx, 1891, p. 235.
Zamenis ladaccensis, Anderson, J. A. S. B. xl, 1871, p. 16.
Zaoccys nigromarginatus (*Coluber*), Blyth, J. A. S. B. xxiii, 1854, p. 290.
Zaoccys tenasserimensis, Sclater, J.A. S. B., lx, 1891, p. 238.
Coluber prasinus, Blyth, J. A. S. B. xxiii, 1854 p. 291.
Pseudoxenodon macrops (*Tropidonotus*), Blyth, J. A. S. B. xxiii, 1854, p. 296.
Tropidonotus platyceps, Blyth, J. A. S. B. xxiii, 1854, p. 297.
Tropidonotus nigrocinctus, Blyth, J. A. S. B. xxiv, 1855, p. 717.
Tropidonotus pealii, Sclater, J. A. S. B., lx, 1891, p. 241.
Tropidonotus nicobarensis, Sclater, J. A. S. B lx, 1891, p. 241.
Dipsas multifasciatus, Blyth, J. A. S. B. xxix, 1860, p. 114.
Dipsas rhinopoma, Blanford, Ann. Mag. N. H. (4) xiv, p. 34.
Hypsirhina maculata, Blanford, J. A. S. B. xlviii, 1879, p. 130.*
Distira tuberculata (*Hydrophis*), Anderson J. A. S. B. xl, 1871, p. 18.
Amblycephalus modestus (*Pareas*), Theobald, Journ. Linn. Soc. x, 1868, p. 55.
Amblycephalus macularius, (*Pareas*), Theobald, Journ. Linn. Soc. x, 1868, p. 54.
Trimeresurus cantoris (*Trigonocephalus*), Blyth, J. A. S. B. xv, 1846, p. 377.

LIST OF THE INDIAN SNAKES NOT REPRESENTED IN THE INDIAN MUSEUM.

Typhlops leucomelas, Boul.
„ oatesi, Boul.
„ mirus, Jan
„ andamanensis, Stol.
„ tenuicollis, (Peters)
Uropeltis grandis, Kel.
Rhinophis punctatus, Müll.
„ planiceps, Peters
Silybura liura, Günth.
„ broughami, Bedd.
„ macrorhynchus, Bedd.
„ phipsoni Mason
Silybura myhendrae, Bedd.
„ madurensis, Bedd.
„ arcticeps, Günth.
„ macrolepis, Peters.
Pseudoplectrurus canaricus, (Bedd.)
Plectrurus davisonii, Bedd.
„ guentheri, Bedd.
„ aureus, Bedd.
Melanophidium wynadense, (Bedd.)
„ punctatum, Bedd.
„ bilineatum, Bedd.
Calamaria catenata, Bly.

* Name changed to blanfordi by Boulenger (Reptiles Brit. Ind. p. 377).

Xylophis stenorhynchus, (Günth.)
Trachischium rubriventer, (Jerd.)
Aspidura copii, Günth.
Haplocercus ceylonensis, Günth.
Lycodon anamallensis, Günth.
„ atropurpureus, Cant.
„ septemtrionalis, (Günth.)
„ carinatus, (Kuhl)
Hydrophobus gracilis, (Günth.)
Pseudocyclophis walteri, Boettg.
„ olivaceus, (Bedd.)
Simotes splendidus, Günth.
„ beddomii, Boul.
„ torquatus, Boul.
Oligodon venustus, (Jerd.)
„ travancoricus, Bedd.
„ brevicauda, Günth.
„ templetonii, Günth.
„ ellioti, Günth.
Lytorhynchus paradoxus, (Günth.)
Zamenis gracilis, Günth.
Coluber frenatus, (Gray)
Dendrophis grandoculis, Boul.
Dendrophis candolineolatus, Günth.
Tropidonotus khasiensis, Boul.
„ ceylonensis, Günth.
„ bellulus, Stol.
„ sancti-johannis, Boul.
Stoliczkaia khasiensis, Jerd.
Dipsas barnesii, Günth.
Psammophis longifrons, Boul.
Hydrophis schistosus, Daud.
„ mamillaris, Daud.
„ spiralis, (Shaw)
„ torquatus, Günth.
Distira stokesii, (Gray).
„ bituberculata, (Peters)
„ ornata, (Gray)
Amblycephalus laevis, Boie
„ andersonii, (Boul.)
Azemiops feae, Boul.
Trimeresurus mucrosquamatus, (Cantor)

SYSTEMATIC INDEX.

(The names of Indian species are printed in small capitals of exotic species in ordinary type.)

OPHIDIA.

	No. of specimens.	page
FAMILY TYPHOPIDAE.		
1 TYPHLOPS BRAMINUS, ...	54	1
2 TYPHLOPS BEDDOMII, ...	1	2
3 TYPHLOPS JERDONI, ...	1	2
4 TYPHLOPS DIARDI, ...	28	2
5 TYPHLOPS BOTHRIORHYNCHUS ...	10	2
6 TYPHLOPS PORRECTUS, ...	1	2
7 TYPHLOPS THEOBALDIANUS,	2	3
8 TYPHLOPS ACUTUS, ...	9	3
9 Typhlops persicus, ...	1	3
10 Typhlops syriacus, ...	2	3
11 Typhlops nigrescens, ...	2	3
12 Typhlina lineata, ...	1	3
13 Feylinia currori, ...	1	3
FAMILY GLAUCONIIDAE.		
14 GLAUCONIA BLANFORDI,	4	4
FAMILY BOIDAE.		
15 Morelia spilotes, ...	5	4
16 Morelia variegata, ...	3	4
17 PYTHON RETICULATUS, ...	15	4
18 PYTHON MOLURUS, ...	12	4
19 Hortulia regia, ...	1	5
20 Aspidiotes melanocephalus, ...	1	5
21 Corallus hortulanus, ...	1	5
22 Epicrates cenchria, ...	2	5
23 Boa constrictor, ...	2	5
24 GONGYLOPHIS CONICUS,...	15	5
25 ERYX JOHNII, ...	11	6
26 Eryx jaculus, ...	8	6
27 Eryx thebaicus, ...	1	6
28 Charina bottae, ...	1	6
FAMILY ILYSIIDAE.		
29 CYLINDROPHIS RUFUS, ...	6	6
30 CYLINDROPHIS MACULATUS,	5	7
FAMILY UROPELTIDAE.		
31 RHINOPHIS OXYRHYNCHUS,	6	7
32 RHINOPHIS TREVELYANUS,	9	7
33 RHINOPHIS SANGUINEUS,	1	7
34 RHINOPHIS BLYTHI, ...	4	7
35 SILYBURA MELANOGASTER,	5	7
36 SILYBURA PULNEYENSIS,	8	7
37 SILYBURA GRANDIS, ...	2	8
38 SILYBURA PETERSII, ...	1	8
39 SILYBURA MACULATA, ...	4	8
40 SILYBURA OCELLATA, ...	9	8
41 SILYBURA NIGRA, ...	2	8
42 SILYBURA NITIDA, ...	2	8
43 SILYBURA DINDIGALENSIS,	1	9
44 SILYBURA ELLIOTI ...	15	9
45 SILYBURA RUBROLINEATA,	1	9

	No. of specimens.	page
46 SILYBURA RUBROMACULATA,	1	9
47 SILYBURA BREVIS, ...	14	9
48 PLECTRURUS PERROTETI,	11	9
49 PLATYPLECTRURUS TRILINEATUS, ...	1	10
50 PLATYPLECTRURUS MADURENSIS, ...	3	10
51 PLATYPLECTRURUS SANGUINEUS ...	3	10

FAMILY XENOPELTIDAE.

	No. of specimens.	page
52 XENOPELTIS UNICOLOR ...	15	10

FAMILY COLUBRIDAE.

SUBFAMILY COLUBRINAE.

	No. of specimens.	page
53 CALAMARIA PAVIMENTATA	1	10
54 Calamaria stahlknechti	1	11
55 Calamaria sumatrana ...	1	11
56 XYLOPHIS PERROTETI ...	5	11
57 TRACHISCHIUM FUSCUM	26	11
58 TRACHISCHIUM GUENTHERI	3	11
59 TRACHISCHIUM TENUICEPS	4	11
60 TRACHISCHIUM MONTICOLA	9	12
61 BLYTHIA RETICULATA ...	8	12
62 ASPIDURA BRACHYORRHOS	12	12
63 ASPIDURA GUENTHERI ...	5	12
64 ASPIDURA TRACHYPROCTA	2	12
65 Virginia striatula ...	1	13
66 Homolosoma lutrix ...	3	13
67 Boodon geometricus ...	1	13
68 Boodon unicolor ...	1	13
69 Boodon lineatus ...	1	13
70 Lamprophis aurora ...	1	13
71 LYCODON STRIATUS ...	7	13
72 LYCODON JARA ...	15	14
73 LYCODON TRAVANCORICUS	6	14
74 LYCODON AULICUS ...	104	14
75 LYCODON FASCIATUS, ...	2	15
76 LYCODON GAMMIEI, ...	1	15
77 Lycodon subcinctus ...	3	16
78 Lycodon effrene, ...	1	16
79 HYDROPHOBUS NYMPHA,	4	16
80 HYDROPHOBUS DAVISONI	2	16
81 Hydrophobus subannulatus ...	1	16
82 PSEUDOCYCLOPHIS BICOLOR, ...	4	16
83 Pseudocyclophis persicus, ...	2	17
84 POLYODONTOPHIS COLLARIS, ...	22	17
85 POLYODONTOPHIS SUBPUNCTATUS ...	5	17
86 POLYODONTOPHIS SAGITTARIUS, ...	16	17
87 POLYODONTOPHIS BISTRIGATUS, ...	2	18
88 Polyodontophis melanocephalus ...	3	18
89 ABLABES CALAMARIA ...	5	18
90 ABLABES STOLICZKAE, ...	2	18
91 ABLABES SCRIPTUS, ...	1	18
92 ABLABES FRENATUS, ...	1	18
93 ABLABES DORIAE, ...	1	18
94 ABLABES RAPPII, ...	11	19
95 ABLABES NICOBARIENSIS,	1	19
96 ABLABES PORPHYRACEUS,	35	19
97 Ablabes modestus, ...	2	19
98 Ablabes collaris, ...	2	19
99 Ablabes fasciatus, ...	1	20
100 Ablabes tricolor, ...	3	20
101 CORONELLA BRACHYURA,	2	20
102 Coronella decorata ...	1	20
103 Coronella cana ...	2	20
104 Coronella phocarum ...	1	20
105 Liophis cobella, ...	4	20
106 Liophis merremii, ...	1	21
107 Liophis reginae ...	1	21
108 Diadophis punctatus, ...	1	21
109 Ophibolus trianguligerus, ...	8	21
110 Ophibolus getulus, ...	2	21
111 Rhinocheilus lecontei,	1	21
112 Cyclophis vernalis, ...	2	21
113 Cyclophis aestivus, ...	3	22
114 Heterodon platyrhinus,	2	22
115 Heterodon dorbignii, ...	2	22
116 Dromicus lineatus, ...	1	22
117 SIMOTES CYCLURUS, ...	30	22
118 SIMOTES ALBOCINCTUS,	52	23
119 SIMOTES PURPURASCENS,	5	23
120 SIMOTES VIOLACEUS. ...	10	23
121 SIMOTES WOODMASONI,	2	24
122 SIMOTES OCTOLINEATUS,	6	24
123 SIMOTES ARNENSIS, ...	15	24
124 SIMOTES THEOBALDI, ...	4	24
125 SIMOTES CRUENTATUS, ...	3	24
126 SIMOTES PLANICEPS, ...	1	25
127 Simotes signatus, ...	1	25
128 OLIGODON AFFINIS, ...	2	25
129 OLIGODON DORSALIS, ...	4	25
130 OLIGODON SUBLINEATUS,	10	25
131 OLIGODON SUBGRISEUS,	29	25
132 Oligodon melanocephalus	2	26
133 Rhagerhis producta, ...	1	26
134 Psammophylax rhombeatus, ...	2	26
135 ZAMENIS KORROS, ...	11	26
136 ZAMENIS MUCOSUS, ...	24	26
137 ZAMENIS VENTRIMACULATUS, ...	16	27

	No. of specimens.	page
138 ZAMENIS LADACCENSIS,	24	27
139 ZAMENIS KARELINI, ...	2	28
140 ZAMENIS FASCIOLATUS,	11	28
141 ZAMENIS DIADEMA, ...	31	28
142 ZAMENIS ARENARIUS, ...	1	29
143 Zamenis ravergieri, ..	13	29
144 Zamenis dahlii, ...	1	29
145 Zamenis hippocrepis ...	3	29
146 ZAOCOYS NIGROMARGINATUS, ...	13	29
147 ZAOCCYS TENASSERIMENSIS, ...	1	30
148 Zaoccys fuscus ...	1	30
149 Salvadora grahamiae ...	1	30
150 Herpetodryas carinatus,	1	30
151 Herpetodryas boddaerti,	1	30
152 Herpetodryas bernieri,	1	30
153 Pityophis melanolencus,	2	30
154 Pityophis catenifer, ...	2	30
155 COLUBER HELENA, ...	25	31
156 COLUBER RETICULARIS,	17	31
157 COLUBER HODGSONII, ...	7	31
158 COLUBER TAENIURUS, ...	6	31
159 COLUBER RADIATUS, ...	24	32
160 COLUBER MELANURUS, ...	7	32
161 COLUBER PRASINUS, ...	10	32
162 COLUBER OXYCEPHALUS,	11	33
163 Coluber subradiatus, ...	1	33
164 Coluber esculapii, ...	1	33
165 Coluber constrictor, ...	5	33
166 Coluber flagelliformis,	3	33
167 Coluber taeniatus, ...	1	33
168 Coluber obsoletus, ...	4	33
169 Coluber guttatus, ...	3	34
170 GONYOPHIS MARGARITATUS, ...	1	34
171 XENELAPHIS HEXAGONATUS, ...	3	34
172 DENDROPHIS PICTUS, ...	86	34
173 DENDROPHIS SUBOCULARIS, ...	1	35
174 DENDROPHIS BIFRENALIS,	1	35
175 Dendrophis puuctulata,	3	35
176 DENDRELAPHIS CAUDOLINEATUS, ...	6	35
177 Ahaetulla smaragdina,	1	35
178 Ahaetulla irregularis, ...	1	36
179 Ahaetulla liocercus, ...	1	36
180 Xeuodon rhabdocephalus,	1	36
181 PSEUDOXENODON MACROPS, ...	27	36
182 TROPIDONOTUS MODESTUS	8	36
183 TROPIDONOTUS PLATYCEPS, ...	27	36
184 TROPIDONOTUS BEDDOMII,	9	37
185 TROPIDONOTUS PARALLELUS, ...	14	37
186 TROPIDONOTUS CHRYSARGUS, ...	14	37
187 TROPIDONOTUS NIGROCINCTUS, ...	9	37
188 TROPIDONOTUS SUBMINIATUS, ...	40	38
189 TROPIDONOTUS HIMALAYANUS, ...	28	38
190 TROPIDONOTUS MONTICOLA, ...	2	39
191 TROPIDONOTUS STOLATUS	85	39
192 TROPIDONOTUS PISCATOR,	70	40
193 TROPIDONOTUS PUNCTULATUS, ...	2	41
194 TROPIDONOTUS PLUMBICOLOR, ...	14	41
195 TROPIDONOTUS VIBAKARI,	1	41
196 TROPIDONOTUS PEALII,	2	41
197 TROPIDONOTUS NICOBARENSIS, ...	1	42
198 Tropidonotus rhodomelas, ...	8	42
199 TROPIDONOTUS TRIANGULIGERUS, ...	5	42
200 Tropidonotus lencomelas,	1	42
201 Tropidonotus conspicillatus, ...	1	42
202 Tropidonotus hydrus, ...	23	42
203 Tropidonotus natrix, ...	10	43
204 Tropidonotus tigrinus,	1	43
205 Tropidonotus vittatus,	2	43
206 Tropidonotus saurita,...	7	43
207 Tropidonotus sirtalis, ...	43	43
208 Tropidonotus sipedon,	13	44
209 Tropidonotus leberis, ...	2	44
210 Storeria occipitomaculata,	2	44
211 Storeria dekayi, ...	4	44
212 HELICOPS SCHISTOSUS,	12	44
213 Uranops angulatus, ...	2	45
214 Hydrops abacurus, ...	1	45
215 Hydrops erythrogrammus, ...	1	45
216 Xenochrophis cerasogaster, ...	5	45
SUBFAMILY DASYPELTINAE.		
217 Dasypeltis scabra, ...	2	45
SUBFAMILY ACROCHORDINAE.		
218 CHERSYDRUS GRANULATUS, ...	3	45
SUBFAMILY DIPSADINAE.		
219 DIPSAS TRIGONATA, ...	23	45
220 DIPSAS CEYLONENSIS, ...	7	46
221 DIPSAS MULTIFASCIATUS,	6	46
222 DIPSAS GOKOOL. ..	12	46
223 DIPSAS MULTIMACULATA,	8	46

	No. of specimens.	page
224 DIPSAS HEXAGONATUS,	34	47
225 DIPSAS CYANEA, ...	3	47
226 DIPSAS CYNODON, ...	8	47
227 DIPSAS FUSCA, ...	5	47
228 DIPSAS FORSTENII, ...	7	47
229 Dipsas rhinopoma, ...	1	48
230 Dipsas boops, ...	1	48
231 Dipsas cenchoa, ...	1	48
232 Leptodeira rufescens, ...	2	48
233 Thamnodynastes natteri, ...	1	48
234 ELACHISTODON WESTERMANNI, ...	1	48
235 Tantilla gracilis, ...	2	48
236 Scytale coronatum, ...	2	49
237 PSAMMODYNASTES PULVERULENTUS, ...	62	49
238 Psammodynastes pictus,	4	49
239 Coelopeltis lacertina, ...	2	49
240 Taphrometopum lineolatum, ...	6	49
241 PSAMMOPHIS LEITHII, ...	18	50
242 PSAMMOPHIS CONDANARUS, ...	7	50
243 Psammophis sibilans, ...	4	50
244 Psammophis crucifer,	1	50
245 Psammophis elegans, ...	2	51
246 DRYOPHIS PERROTETI, ...	5	51
247 DRYOPHIS DISPAR, ...	2	51
248 DRYOPHIS FRONTICINCTUS, ...	3	51
249 DRYOPHIS PRASINUS, ...	42	51
250 DRYOPHIS MYCTERIZANS,	27	52
251 DRYOPHIS PULVERULENTUS, ...	7	52
252 Dryophis acuminata, ...	1	52
253 Bucephalus capensis, ...	2	52
254 CHRYSOPELEA ORNATA,	33	53
255 Chrysopelea rubescens,	1	53
SUBFAMILY HOMALOPSINAE.		
256 HOMALOPSIS BUCCATA, ...	5	53
357 CERBERUS RHYNCHOPS, ...	53	54
258 HYPSIRHINA PLUMBEA, ...	8	54
259 HYPSIRHINA ENHYDRIS,	31	54
260 HYPSIRHINA BLANFORDI,	1	55
261 HYPSIRHINA SIEBOLDII,	5	55
262 Hypsirhina bennetti, ...	1	55
263 FORDONIA LEUCOBALIA,	6	55
264 GERARDIA PREVOSTIANA,	8	55
265 CANTORIA VIOLACEA, ...	2	55
266 HIPISTES HYDRINUS, ...	11	56
SUBFAMILY ELAPINAE.		
267 CALLOPHIS TRIMACULATUS, ...	1	56
268 CALLOPHIS MACULICEPS,	5	56
269 CALLOPHIS NIGRESCENS,	6	56
270 CALLOPHIS MACLELLANDI, ...	11	56
271 CALLOPHIS BIBRONI, ...	1	57
272 Callophis gracilis, ...	1	57
273 Adenophis bivirgatus,	4	57
274 ADENOPHIS INTESTINALIS, ...	7	57
275 MEGAEROPHIS FLAVICEPS, ...	1	57
276 BUNGARUS FASCIATUS, ...	12	57
277 BUNGARUS CEYLONICUS,	2	58
278 BUNGARUS CAERULEUS,	21	58
279 BUNGARUS BUNGAROIDES,	4	58
280 BUNGARUS LIVIDUS, ...	3	58
281 Bungarus semifasciatus,	2	58
282 NAIA TRIPUDIANS, ...	54	59
283 NAIA BUNGARUS, ...	8	59
284 Diemenia olivacea, ...	1	60
285 Diemenia reticulata, ...	1	60
286 Pseudechis porphyriacus,	3	60
287 Brachysoma diadema,	1	60
288 Hoplocephalus gouldii,	2	60
289 Cacophis harrietae, ...	1	60
290 Acanthophis antarcticus,	4	60
291 Elaps fulvius, ...	2	61
292 Elaps nigrocinctus, ...	3	61
293 Elaps lemniscatus, ...	2	61
294 Elaps hygiae, ...	2	61
295 Vermicella annulata, ...	6	61
SUBFAMILY HYDROPHINAE.		
296 PLATURUS LATICAUDATUS,	2	61
297 PLATURUS COLUBRINUS,	4	62
298 ENHYDRIS CURTUS, ...	1	62
299 ENHYDRIS HARDWICKII,	13	62
300 HYDRUS PLATURUS, ...	8	62
301 HYDROPHIS CAERULESCENS, ...	7	62
302 HYDROPHIS NIGROCINCTUS,	2	63
303 HYDROPHIS LATIFASCIATUS,	1	63
304 HYDROPHIS CORONATUS,	5	63
305 HYDROPHIS OBSCURUS, ...	6	63
306 HYDROPHIS FASCIATUS,	7	63
307 HYDROPHIS GRACILIS, ...	7	64
308 HYDROPHIS CANTORIS, ...	9	64
309 Hydrophis elegans, ...	1	64
310 ENHYDRINA VALAKADIEN,	45	64
311 DISTIRA JERDONI, ...	7	65
312 DISTIRA ROBUSTA, ...	16	65
313 DISTIRA TUBERCULATA,	1	65
314 DISTIRA CYANOCINCTA, ...	19	65
315 DISTIRA LAPEMIDOIDES,	19	66
316 DISTIRA VIPERINA, ...	6	66

	No. of specimens.	page
FAMILY AMBLYCEPHALIDAE.		
317 AMBLYCEPHALUS MONTICOLA, ...	8	66
318 AMBLYCEPHALUS MODESTUS, ...	1	66
319 AMBLYCEPHALUS MACULARIUS, ...	3	67
320 AMBLYCEPHALUS CARINATUS, ...	8	67
321 AMBLYCEPHALUS MOELLENDORFFII, ...	1	67
322 Leptognathus nebulatus,	1	67
FAMILY VIPERIDAE.		
SUBFAMILY VIPERINAE.		
323 VIPERA RUSSELLII, ...	70	67
324 VIPERA LEBETINA, ...	3	68
325 Vipera ammodytes, ...	2	61
326 Pelias berus, ...	12	68
327 Cerastes hasselquisti, ...	1	68
328 Cerastes persious, ...	1	68
329 Clotho arietans, ...	1	68
330 ECHIS CARINATA, ...	29	69
331 Atheris squamata, ...	1	69
SUBFAMILY CROTALINAE,		
332 ANCISTRODON HIMALAYANUS, ...	12	69
333 ANCISTRODON HYPNALE,	14	70
334 Ancistrodon pallasii, ...	2	70
335 Ancistrodon contortrix.	3	70
336 TRIMERESURUS MONTICOLA, ...	20	70
337 TRIMERESURUS STRIGATUS, ...	4	70
338 TRIMERESURUS JERDONII,	1	71
339 TRIMERESURUS CANTORIS,	20	71
340 TRIMERESURUS PURPUREOMACULATUS, ...	72	71
341 TRIMERESURUS GRAMINEUS, ...	79	72
342 TRIMERESURUS ANAMALLENSIS, ...	16	73
343 TRIMERESURUS TRIGONOCEPHALUS, ...	1	73
344 TRIMERESURUS MACROLEPIS, ...	2	73
345 Trimeresurus wagleri,	1	73
346 Craspedocephalns atrox,	2	73
347 Craspedocephalus bilineatus, ...	1	73
348 Crotalus adamanteus, ...	4	74
349 Crotalus horridus, ...	1	74
350 Crotalus miliarius, ...	1	74

LIST OF THE SNAKES

IN THE

INDIAN MUSEUM.

Family TYPHLOPIDAE.

1. TYPHLOPS BRAMINUS, (Daud.).

Boulenger, p. 236.

Distribution—Indian Empire, South China, Malay Peninsula and Islands, S. Africa and Madagascar.

1 Afghanistan	Boundary Commission	12896.
1 Rajanpur	Dr. C. Saunders	6898.
1 Ajmere	Sir O. B. C. St. John	13482.
4 Allahabad	John Cockburn	6892, 6910, 6931-2.
3 Upper Godavery dist., C. P.	Dr. Geoffrey	6904-6.
5 Anamalai Hills, Mdr.	Col. R. H. Beddome	4411-2, 4444-6.
1 Tinnevelli Hills, Mdr.	Col. R. H. Beddome	4442.
1 Travancore	Col. R. H. Beddome	2846.
1 Colombo, Ceylon	W. Ferguson	6882.
2 Ceylon	H. Nevill	8744-5.
2 Monghyr	E. Lockwood	6929-30.
1 Darbhangah	C. Maries	11936.
1 Rajmahal	Purchased	10979.
1 Serampore	Genl. G. B. Mainwaring	12635.
4 Calcutta	Museum Collector	6952, 11409, 13229-30.
1 Calcutta	J. Anderson	6891.
3 Calcutta	J. Wood Mason	12869, 1323-4.
1 Calcutta	R. D'Cruz	11861.
1 Calcutta	C. Cadell	11355.
1 Calcutta	B. Manger	12717.
4 Zoological Gardens, Calcutta	J. Anderson	11952, 11461-3.
3 Botanical Gardens, Calcutta	J. Anderson	6911-3.
1 Haldibari, Kuch Behar	Purchased	10990.
1 Goalpara, Assam	No history	6887.
2 Sibsagar „	S. E. Peal	6862-3.
1 Naga hills „	Capt. J. Butler	6917.
1 Durrang, Duffla hills	Col. H. H. Godwin Austen	4006.
2 Assam	F. Stoliczka, [Ex.]	6880-1.
2 Silcuri, Cachar	J. Wood Mason	12041, 12043.
1 Proome, Burma	J. Anderson	4145.

2. TYPHLOPS BEDDOMII, Boul.

Boulenger, p. 237.
Distribution—Hills of the Peninsula of India.

1 Travancore	Col. R. H. Beddome	4377.

3. TYPHLOPS JERDONI, Boul.

Boulenger, p. 238.
Distribution—The Bhutan Doars and Assam hills.

1 Buxa, Doars	Museum Coll. (Moti Ram)	12566.

4. TYPHLOPS DIARDI, Schleg.

Boulenger, p. 238; Sclater, J. A. S. B. lx. p. 232.
Distribution—Bengal, Sikkim, Assam, Burma, Cochin China and Malay Peninsula.

1 Botanical Gardens, Calcutta	J. Anderson	6860.
2 Jira, Garo hills, Assam	Capt. Williamson	3946, 6901.
1 Shillong, Assam	Col. H. H. Godwin Austen	4002.
8 Sibsagar, Assam	S. E. Peal	4047-8, 6857, 6861, 6864, 6907, 6922, 6934.
2 Nazira, Sibsagar Dist.	J. M. Foster	6855, 6933.
3 Samaguting, Assam	Capt. J. Butler	6856, 6900, 6925.
2 Dilcoosh, N. Cachar	J. Inglis	11358-9.
1 Cachar	Mus. Coll.	6858.
1 Cachar	Purchased	6897.
1 Pegu	W. Theobald	6859.
1 Moulmein	W. Theobald	6879.
	(TYPE OF T. BARMANUS, Stoliczka).	
1 Johore, Malay P.	J. Wood Mason	4240.
1 (from stomach of Athene brama)	J. Anderson	6865.
1 No loc.	F. Stoliczka	4454.
2 No loc.	A. S. B.	6851, 6853.

5. TYPHLOPS BOTHRIORHYNCHUS, Gunth.

Boulenger, p. 239; Sclater, J. A. S. B. lx, p. 232.
Distribution—N. India, Assam and Malay Peninsula.

1 Garo hills	N. Belletty	6854.
3 Sibsagar, Assam	S. E. Peal	6866, 6921, 6923.
2 Samaguting, Assam	Capt. J. Butler	6894, 6928.
2 Silcuri, Cachar	J. Wood Mason	12040, 12042.
1 No loc.	A. S. B.	6852.
1 No loc.	No history	6896.

6. TYPHLOPS PORRECTUS, Stol.

Boulenger, p. 240.
Distribution—Himalayas and Northern India.

1 Amber N. E. of Murree	F. Stoliczka (Yarkand Exped.)	6916.

7. TYPHLOPS THEOBALDIANUS, Stol.

Boulenger, p. 240; Sclater, J. A. S. B. lx, p. 232.
Distribution—Assam.

1 Samaguting, Assam	Capt. J. Butler	8723.
1 No loc.	A. S. B.	6888.

(TYPE OF THE SPECIES, Stoliczka.)

8. TYPHLOPS ACUTUS, (Dum. & Bibr.).

Boulenger, p. 241; Sclater, J. A. S. B. lx, p. 232.
Distribution—The Bengal and Madras Presidencies.

1 Sipri, Gwalior	F. J. Daly	13235.
1 Deccan	No history	6940.
1 Malabar	E. Gerard [P.]	12422.
1 Chybassa	Major H. L. Haughton	6939.
1 Balasore dist.	J. Cleghorn	13399.
1 Calcutta	Babu P. C. Bysack	6937.
1 Calcutta	Babu Protab Chunder	6938.
2 Kishnaghur	R. de Dombal	6935, 6.

9. TYPHLOPS PERSICUS, Blanf.

Blanford, Persia, p. 399.
Distribution—Persia.

1 N. E. of Sarjan nr. Shiraz	W. T. Blanford	6899.

(TYPE OF THE SPECIES, Blanford.)

10. TYPHLOPS SYRIACUS, Jan.

Jan, Icon. Ophid., p. 15.
Distribution—Palestine and Syria.

1 nr Galilee, Palestine	J. Anderson	11113.
1 Mt. Hermon	J. Anderson	11152.

11. TYPHLOPS NIGRESCENS, (Gray).

Krefft, Austr. Snakes, p. 18.
Distribution—Eastern Australia.

2 Queensland	Brisbane Mus. [Ex.]	11870, 11872.

12. TYPHLINA LINEATA, (Boie).

Gunther, Reptiles Brit. Ind., p. 171.
Distribution—Malay Peninsula, Sumatra, Borneo and Java.

1 Borneo	E. Gerard, [P.]	12476.

13. FEYLINIA CURRORI, Gray.

Gray, Cat. Lizards B. M., p. 129.
Distribution—Africa.

1 "Africa"	Berlin Mus. [Ex.]	7920.

Family GLAUCONIIDAE.

14. GLAUCONIA BLANFORDI, Boul.

Boulenger, p. 243.
Distribution—Sind.

4 Karachi ?	J. A. Murray	12014-7.

Family BOIDAE.

15. MORELIA SPILOTES, Gray.

Krefft, Austr. Snakes, p. 29.
Distribution—Parts of New South Wales.

1 Queensland ?	Brisbane Mus. [Ex.]	11884.
2 N. S. Wales ?	Calcutta Exhibition	12622-3.
1 N. S. Wales	G. Nevill	12034.
1 Australia	E. Gerard [P.]	12369.

16. MORELIA VARIEGATA, Gray.

Krefft, Austr. Snakes, p. 31.
Distribution—Australia and New Guinea.

1 New Guinea	E. Gerard [P.]	12377.
1 Queensland	Brisbane Mus. [Ex.]	11883.
1 N. S. Wales ?	Calcutta Exhibition	12621.

17. PYTHON RETICULATUS, (Schneid.).

Boulenger, p. 242.
Distribution—Burma, Nicobar Isles, Malay Peninsula and Islands.

1 Taing, King Isle, Mergui	Mergui Exped. (Anderson)	11554.
1 Lampee or Sullivan Isle, Mergui	Mergui Exped. (Anderson)	11555.
1 Mergui	Major Berdmore, A. S. B.	8042.
1 Nicobars	Col. R. C. Tytler	8040.
4 Nicobars	F. A. de Roepstorff	8045, 12543, 12594-5.
1 Malacca	Rev. W. E. Lindstedt A. S. B.	8044.
3 Johore	J. Meldrum	4647-9.
3 No loc.	No hist.	8046, 8055, 8081.

18. PYTHON MOLURUS, (Linn.).

Boulenger, p. 246; Sclater, J. A. S. B. lx, p. 232.
Distribution—India and Ceylon, Assam, the Malay Peninsula, Java and South China.

1 Sibsagar, Assam	S. E. Peal	4014.
3 Samaguting	Capt. J. Butler	8066, 8068, 8884.
1 Wellesley Prov.	F. Stoliczka	8053.
1 Haiphong, China	Dr. Hungerford	11390.

1 India	Rev. H. J. Harrison	8687.
1 No loc.	W. Rutledge	12611.
1 No loc.	No hist. A. S. B.	8050.
3 No loc.	No hist.	8052, 8054, 8067.
2 (Eggs laid in Calcutta)		8063-4.
(Tongue)		8051.
(Heart, Kidney, Ovary)		8057-9.

19. HORTULIA REGIA, (Shaw).

Gray, Cat. Snakes B. M., p. 90.
Distribution—Africa.

1 W. Africa	E. Gerard, [P.]	12382.

20. ASPIDIOTES MELANOCEPHALUS, Krefft.

Krefft, Austr. Snakes, p. 33.
Distribution—Queensland.

1 Queensland	Brisbane Mus.	11876.

21. CORALLUS HORTULANUS, (Linn.).

Gray, Cat. Snakes B. M., p. 97.
Distribution—West Indies and Tropical South America.

1 South America	Netley Mus. [Ex.]	8626.

22. EPICRATES CENCHRIA, Gray.

Gray, Cat. Snakes B. M., p. 95.
Distribution—West Indies and Tropical South America.

1 West Indies	Netley Mus. [Ex.]	8625.
1 Venezuela	E. Gerard, [P.]	12373.

23. BOA CONSTRICTOR, Linn.

Gray, Cat. Snakes B. M., p. 100.
Distribution—Tropical South America.

2 South America	E. Blyth, A. S. B.	8069-70.

24. GONGYLOPHIS CONICUS, (Schneid.).

Boulenger, p. 247.
Distribution—Throughout India.

1 Allahabad	J. Cockburn	8076.
3 Upper Provinces	No history, A. S. B.	8071, 8073-4.
2 Nowgong, C. P.	F. Daly	13277-8.
3 Anamalai hills	Col. R. H. Beddome	4435-6, 8079.
1 Chandbally, Cuttack dist.	J. Wood Mason	4123.
1 Singbhum	V. Ball	8194.
1 Manbhum	W. Theobald	8080.
1 Chota Nagpur	V. Ball	8077.

1 No loc.	F. Stoliczka	8658.
1 No loc.	J. Wood Mason	12053.

25. ERYX JOHNII, (Russell).

Boulenger, p. 248.
Distribution—Southern and Western India.

1 Rajanpur, Pjb.	Dr. R. C. Sanders	8697.
1 Pind Dadun Khan	W. Theobald, A. S. B.	8085.
1 Ajmere, Rjpt.	Sir O. B. C. St. John	13492.
2 Jeypore	R. Pattoon	8755-6.
1 Rajpootana	N. Belletty	13384.
2 Karachi	Karachi Mus. [Ex.]	8696, 8698.
1 Sind	J. A. Murray	12001.
2 Agra	Agra Mus.	8088-9.

26. ERYX JACULUS, (Linn.).

Blanford, Persia, p. 401.
Distribution—South-east Europe, Western Asia and North-east Africa.

1 Egypt.	Berlin Mus. [Ex.]	7910.
1 Jaffa, Palestine	Berlin Mus. [Ex.]	7911.
1 Kohrud nr. Ispahan	Persian Coll., (Blanford)	3495.
1 Saidabad, S. W. of Karman	Persian Coll., (Blanford)	3496.
4 Bala Morghab, Herat	Afghan B. Comm. (Aitchison)	13141-4.

27. ERYX THEBAICUS, Reuss.

Gray, Cat. Snakes B. M., p. 109.
Distribution—North-East Africa.

1 Egypt.	Berlin Mus. [Ex.]	7909.

28. CHARINA BOTTAE, (Blainville).

Garman, N. Amer. Snakes, p. 7.
Distribution—Throughout the United States.

1 Texas.	Dr. J. H. Garnier, [Ex.]	12164.

Family ILYSIIDAE.

29. CYLINDROPHIS RUFUS, (Laur.).

Boulenger, p. 250.
Distribution—Burma, Cochin China, Malay Peninsula and Islands.

1 Ava, Burma	Yunan Exped. (Anderson)	4003.
1 Proome, Burma	Yunan Exped. (Anderson)	4004.
1 Amherst, Tenasserim	Purchased	7018.
1 Singapore	Raffles Museum, (Davison)	13305.
1 Johore	J. Meldrum	4658.
1 No loc.	A. S. B.	7019.

30. CYLINDROPHIS MACULATUS, (Linn.).

Boulenger, p. 251.
Distribution—Ceylon.

1 Ceylon	H. Nevill	6994.
1 Ceylon	Col. R. H. Beddome	4399.
1 Ceylon	Dr. E. F. Kelaart, A. S. B.	7015.
1 West Prov., Ceylon	W. Ferguson	7016.
1 No loc.	E. Gerard [P.]	12400.

Family UROPELTIDAE.

31. RHINOPHIS OXYRHYNCHUS, (Schneid.).

Boulenger, p. 255.
Distribution—Central Provinces of Ceylon.

6 Ceylon	H. Nevill	6993, 6978, 6980-3.

32. RHINOPHIS TREVELYANUS, (Kelaart).

Boulenger, p. 256.
Distribution—Central Provinces of Ceylon.

1 Kandy, Ceylon	Dr. E. F. Kelaart, A. S. B.	6941.
7 Ceylon	H. Nevill	6984-90.
1 No loc.	Col. R. H. Beddome	8388.

33. RHINOPHIS SANGUINEUS, Beddome.

Boulenger, p. 256.
Distribution—Western Ghats of South India.

1 Tinnevelli hills	Col. R. H. Beddome	6995.

34. RHINOPHIS BLYTHI, Kelaart.

Boulenger, p. 256.
Distribution—Central Provinces of Ceylon.

1 Kandy, Ceylon	Dr. E. F. Kelaart, A. S. B.	6945.
2 Ceylon	H. Nevill	6979, 6992.
1 No loc.	Col. R. H. Beddome	6955.

35. SILYBURA MELANOGASTER, (Gray).

Boulenger, p. 260.
Distribution—Central Provinces of Ceylon.

1 Peradenia, Ceylon	W. Ferguson	6942.
2 Kandy, Ceylon	Dr. E. F. Kelaart, A. S. B.	6946-7.
1 No loc.	Col. R. H. Beddome	4441.
1 No loc.	E. Gerard [P.]	12452.

36. SILYBURA PULNEYENSIS, (Beddome).

Boulenger, p. 260.
Distribution—Hills of Madura dist., S. India.

1 Palni hills	E. Gerard [P.]	12423.
1 Palni hills	Col. R. H. Beddome [Ex.]	6948.
1 No loc.	Col. R. H. Beddome	6950.
	(A TYPICAL SPECIMEN. Beddome.)	
5 No loc.	Col. R. H. Beddome	6972-6976.

37. SILYBURA GRANDIS, (Beddome).

Boulenger, p. 261.
Distribution—Anamalai hills, S. India.

1 Anamalai hills	Col. R. H. Beddome	12412.
1 No loc.	Col. R. H. Beddome	8753.

38. SILYBURA PETERSII, Beddome.

Boulenger, p. 261.
Distribution—Anamalai hills, S. India.

1 Anamalai hills	E. Gerard [P.]	12418.

39. SILYBURA MACULATA, Beddome.

Boulenger, p. 261.
Distribution—Anamalai hills, Sonthern India.

3 Anamalai hills	Col. R. H. Beddome	7000, 7005-6.
1 No loc.	E. Gerard [P.]	12409.

40. SILYBURA OCELLATA, Beddome.

Boulenger, p. 262.
Distribution—Hills of Southern India.

1 Wynaad	E. Gerard [P.]	12414.
1 Nilgiri hills	Col. R. H. Beddome	6959.
4 Anamalai hills	E. Gerard [P.]	12411, 13, 15, 19.
3 No loc.	Col. R. H. Beddome	4308-10.

41. SILYBURA NIGRA, Beddome.

Boulenger, p. 263; Sclater, J. A. S. B. lx, p. 232.
Distribution—Hills of Southern India.

1 Palni hills, 5000 ft.	Col. R. H. Beddome	6953.
1 Palni hills	Col. R. H. Beddome	8760.
	(TYPE OF S. WOODMASONI, Theob.)	

42. SILYBURA NITIDA, Beddome.

Boulenger, p. 263.
Distribution—Anamalai hills, S. India.

1 Anamalai hills, 5000 ft.	Col. R. H. Beddome	6951.
1 Anamalai hills	E. Gerard [P.]	12417.

43. SILYBURA DINDIGALENSIS, Beddome.

Boulenger, p. 264.
Distribution—Hills of the Madura district.

1 Sirumali hills, Madura dist., 4000 ft.	Col. R. H. Beddome [Ex.]	6960.

44. SILYBURA ELLIOTI, Gray.

Boulenger, p. 265.
Distribution—Eastern and Western Ghats and Hills of S. India.

1 Ganjam hills	Col. R. H. Beddome	7001.
4 Colegal hills, Coimb. dist.	Col. R. H. Beddome	6961-4.
1 Anamalai hills	Col. R. H. Beddome	6998.
2 Anamalai hills	Dr. T. C. Jerdon	7834-5.
1 South Arcot dist.	Museum Collector	13270.
3 Tinnevelli hills	Col. R. H. Beddome	4410, 6997, 6999.
3 No loc.	Col. R. H. Beddome	6967-8.

45. SILYBURA RUBROLINEATA, Gunth.

Boulenger, p. 266.
Distribution—Anamalai and Travancore hills.

1 Anamalai hills	Col. R. H. Beddome, [Ex.]	7833.

46. SILYBURA RUBROMACULATA, Beddome.

Boulenger, p. 268.
Distribution—Anamalai hills, Southern India.

1 Anamalai hills	E. Gerard [P.]	12416.

47. SILYBURA BREVIS, Gunth.

Boulenger, p. 268; Sclater, J. A. S. B. lx, p. 232.
Distribution—Hills of Ganjam dist. and of Southern India.

1 Ganjam hills	Col. R. H. Beddome	7002.
1 Shevaroy hills	Col. R. H. Beddome	6966.
2 Nilliampati, Anamalai hills	E. Gerard [P.]	12406-7.
1 Anamalai hills	Col. R. H. Beddome	7004.
1 Anamalai hills	E. Gerard [P.]	12410.
1 Madamelly, Malabar	Col. R. H. Beddome	7573.
2 Madras Presidency	Col. R. H. Beddome	3200, 6971.
1 South India	E. Gerard [P.]	12408.
4 No loc.	Col. R. H. Beddome	4305-7, 6954.

48. PLECTRURUS PERROTETI, Dum. & Bibr.

Boulenger, p. 271.
Distribution—Anamalai and Nilgiri hills of S. India.

4 Ootacamund, Nilgiris	W. Theobald, A. S. B.	7011-14.
3 Nilgiris	T. C. Jerdon	7008-10.
1 Nilgiris	E. A. Minchin	12951.

2 Madras Pr.	W. Davison	6958, 6965.
1 No loc.	E. Gerard [P.]	12424.

49. PLATYPLECTRURUS TRILINEATUS, (Beddome)

Boulenger, p. 274.
Distribution—Anamalai hills, S. India.

1 No loc.	Col. R. H. Beddome, [Ex.]	7083.

50. PLATYPLECTRURUS MADURENSIS, Beddome.

Boulenger p. 274.
Distribution—Palni and Travancore hills, S. India.

1 Palni hills	E. Gerard [P.]	12420.

51. PLATYPLECTRURUS SANGUINEUS, (Beddome)

Boulenger, p. 274.
Distribution—Anamalai hills, Wynaad and Travancore.

1 Anamalai hills	Col. R. H. Beddome	6996.
1 Anamalai hills	E. Gerard [P.]	12421.
1 Madras Presidency	Col. R. H. Beddome	7007.

Family XENOPELTIDAE.

52. XENOPELTIS UNICOLOR, Reinw.

Boulenger, p. 276.
Distribution—S. India, Burma, Indo-China, Malay Peninsula and Islands.

1 Trichinopoli, S. Ind.	H. F. Blanford, A. S. B.	8035.
2 Pegu	W. Theobald	8038-9.
2 Pegu	Major Berdmore, A. S. B.	8031-2.
1 Proome	Yunan Exped. (Anderson)	4202.
1 Tavoy	Mus. Collector	12834.
1 Mergui	Mergui Exped. (Anderson)	11572.
1 Burma	Capt. Hood	8037.
1 Singapore	Capt. T. S. Gardiner	12640.
4 Singapore	Derrick Spon	12963-66.
1 No loc.	F. Stoliczka	3956.

Family COLUBRIDAE.

Sub-family COLUBRINAE.

53. CALAMARIA PAVIMENTATA, Dum. & Bibr.

Boulenger, p. 282.
Distribution—Burma, South China, Indo-China, Malay Peninsula and Islands.

1 Johore, Malay P.	Museum Collector	4450.

54. CALAMARIA STAHLNECHTI, Stol.

Stoliczka, J. A. S. B. xlii, p. 119.
Distribution—Malay Peninsula.

1 Penang	F. Stoliczka	7122.

(TYPE OF THE SPECIES, Stoliczka)

55. CALAMARIA SUMATRANA, Edeling.

Sclater, J. A. S. B. lx, p. 233.
Distribution—Malay Peninsula and Sumatra.

1 Singapore	Raffles Museum (W. Davison)	13306.

56. XYLOPHIS PERROTETI, (Dum. & Bibr.)

Boulenger, p. 283.
Distribution—Hills of Southern India.

1 Nilgiri hills, Md. Pr.	Dr. T. C. Jerdon	7017.
1 Anamalai hills, Md. Pr.	Col. R. H. Beddome	4440.
1 Milamullay, Md. Pr.	Col. R. H. Beddome	7020.
1 Tinnevelli hills, Md. Pr.	Col. R. H. Beddome	4395.
1 South India.	E. Gerard [P.]	12393.

57. TRACHISCHIUM FUSCUM, (Bly.).

Boulenger, p. 285.
Distribution—Sikkim and Burma ?

11 Darjeeling	Major W. S. Sherwill, A. S. B.	7043-53.

(TYPES OF THE SPECIES, Blyth).

3 Darjeeling	Major W. S. Sherwill and W. Theobald, A. S. B.	7038-40.
3 Darjeeling	J. Gammie	7063-5.
1 Darjeeling	E. T. Atkinson	13290.
1 Darjeeling	J. Anderson	7062.
1 Darjeeling	W. S. Atkinson	8529.
2 Darjeeling	J. S. Gamble	12024-5.
1 Gompahar forest, Darjeeling, 7,500 ft.	J. S. Gamble	12022.
1 "Rangoon"	Purchased, A. S. B.	7042.
1 No loc.	No history, A. S. B.	7057.
1 No loc.	No history	7058.

58. TRACHISCHIUM GUENTHERI, Boul.

Boulenger, p. 285 ; Sclater, J. A. S. B. lx, p. 233.
Distribution—Nepal and Sikkim ?

1 Khatmandu, Nepal	Museum Collector	7033.
2 "Allahabad"	J. Cockburn	8763-4.

59. TRACHISCHIUM TENUICEPS, (Bly.).

Boulenger, p. 286.
Distribution—Sikkim.

1 Darjeeling	Major W. S. Sherwill, A. S. B.	7181.

(TYPE OF THE SPECIES, Blyth).

1 Darjeeling	J. Anderson	7031.
2 Darjeeling	J. Gammie	7034, 8820.

60. TRACHISCHIUM MONTICOLA, (Cantor).

Boulenger, p. 286.
Distribution—Sikkim and Assam.

4 Dikrang, Assam	Duffla Exped. (H. H. Godwin Austen)	4101-3, 8530.
2 Charapunji, „	J. H. Bourne	8559-60.
1 Sibsagar, „	S. E. Peal	4045.
1 Naga hills „	Capt. H. Butcher	8647.
1 "Barrakur"	G. Nevill	7180.

61. BLYTHIA RETICULATA, (Bly.).

Boulenger, p. 287.
Distribution—Hills of Assam.

1 Shillong, Assam	Duffla Exped. (H. H. Godwin Austen)	4004.
2 Charapunji, „	J. H. Bourne	7060-1.
3 Samagooting, „	Capt. J. Butler	7054-6.
2 Assam	W. Robinson, A. S. B.	7028-9.

(Types of the species, Blyth.)

62. ASPIDURA BRACHYORRHOS, (Boie).

Boulenger, p. 289.
Distribution—Ceylon highlands.

1 Kadriganam, Ceylon	E. F. Kelaart, A. S. B.	7026.
1 Ceylon (30 m. e. of Columbo)	W. Ferguson	7024.
1 Ceylon	Col. R. H. Beddome	4423.
9 No loc.	Col. R. H. Beddome	8390-8.

63. ASPIDURA GUENTHERI, Ferguson.

Boulenger, p. 290.
Distribution—Ceylon coast-lands.

3 Ceylon	W. Ferguson	7021-3.
2 Ceylon	A. C. L. Günther	8684-5.

64. ASPIDURA TRACHYPROCTA, Cope.

Boulenger, p. 290.
Distribution—Ceylon highlands.

1 Kambaddy, Ceylon	W. Ferguson	7015.
1 No loc.	Col. R. H. Beddome	4424.

65. VIRGINIA STRIATULA, (Linn.).

Garman, N. Amer. Snakes, p. 97.
Distribution—Eastern States of North America.

1 N. America	Purchased	7027.

(TYPE OF FALCONERIA BENGALENSIS, Theobald).

66. HOMALOSOMA LUTRIX, (Linn.).

Günther, Cat. Col. Snakes, p. 20.
Distribution—South Africa.

1 Malmesbury, S. Africa	Berlin Mns. [Ex.]	7917.
1 Natal	Netley Mus.	8636.
1 S. Africa	Purchased, A. S. B.	7208.

(TYPE OF CYCLOPHIS CATENATUS, Theobald.)

67. BOODON GEOMETRICUS, (Schleg.).

Günther, Cat. Col. Snakes, p. 198.
Distribution—West Africa.

1 S. W. Africa	Netley Mus.	8463.

68. BOODON UNICOLOR, (Schleg.).

Günther, Cat. Col. Snakes, p. 199.
Distribution—West Africa.

1 Accra, W. Africa	Berlin Mus. [Ex.]	7912.

69. BOODON LINEATUS, Dum. & Bibr.

Günther, Cat. Col. Snakes, p. 199.
Distribution—West and South Africa.

1 Africa	E. Gerard [P.]	12359.

70. LAMPROPHIS AURORA, (Linn.).

Günther, Cat. Col. Snakes, p. 195.
Distribution—S. Africa.

1 S. Africa	G. E. Dobson [Ex.]	8769.

71. LYCODON STRIATUS, (Shaw).

Boulenger, p. 292; Sclater, J. A. S. B. lx, p. 233.
Distribution—Northern India from Sind to Ganjam.

1 Hills below Simla	F. Stoliczka [P.]	7975.
1 Ajmere, Rjpt.	Sir O. B. C. St. John	13488.
1 Jemper, Sind	Karachi Mus. [Ex.]	8406.
1 Lahore	Sir J. Fayrer	} 7973-4.
1 Agra	Agra Museum	
1 Aska, Ganjam dist.	E. A. Minchin	12941.
1 Ganjam	V. Ball	7976.

72. LYCODON JARA, (Shaw).

Boulenger, p. 292.
Distribution—Bengal, Assam and Pegu ; Anamalai hills ?

1 Botanical Gardens, Calcutta	J. Anderson	8015.
1 Calcutta	J. Anderson	8943.
1 Tura, Garo hills, Assam	O. L. Fraser	13203.
1 Garo hills, "	Col. H. H. Godwin Austen	8018.
1 Charapunji, "	Lieut. Bourne	8016.
2 Sibsagar, "	S. E. Peal	4044, 8017.
1 Nazira, "	J. M. Foster	4131.
1 Dilcosh, N. E. Cachar	J. Inglis	11364.
2 Cachar	Museum Coll. 1868	8013-4.
4 No loc.	No history, A. S. B.	8007, 8010-12.

73. LYCODON TRAVANCORICUS, (Beddome).

Boulenger, p. 293 ; Sclater, J. A. S. B. lx, p. 233.
Distribution—Hills of Southern India.

1 Conoor, Nilgiri hills	F. Daly	13396.
2 S. Arcot dist.	Museum Coll.	13271-2.
2 Tinnevelli hills	Col. R. H. Beddome	4425, 7576.
1 No loc.	Col. R. H. Beddome	4419.

74. LYCODON AULICUS, (Linn.).

Boulenger, p. 294.
Distribution—India from the Himalayas to Ceylon, Assam, Burma, Indo-China, Malay Peninsula and Islands.

1 Khatmandu, Nepal	W. Whitwell	11403.
2 Darjeeling	J. Anderson	8945-6.
2 Jeypore, Rjpt.	R. Pattoon	8451-2.
1 Ajmere, Rjpt.	Sir O. B. C. St. John	13481.
3 Agra	Agra Museum	7997-9.
1 Allahabad	J. Cockburn	7972.
1 Goruckpore	A. C. L. Carlleylo	4678.
2 Nowgong, C. P.	F. J. Daly	13280, 13415.
1 Bangalore	E. A. Minchin	12940.
1 Dindigal hills, S. Ind.	Col. R. H. Beddome	4401.
1 Anamalai hills	Col. R. H. Beddome	4447.
2 South India	Dr. T. C. Jerdon, A. S. B.	7950-1.
1 Colombo, Ceylon	W. Ferguson	7977.
1 Ceylon	W. Ferguson	7968.
2 Ceylon	E. F. Kelaart, A. S. B.	7952-3.
1 Ganjam dist.	E. A. Minchin	12938.
2 Singbhum	V. Ball	8002-3.
1 Monghyr	E. Lockwood, A. S. B.	8578.
1 Doomerkoonda (Ranigunj)	J. S. Buchanan	7966.
1 Hooghly (double headed)	Dr. R. F. Thomson	7965.
6 Calcutta	E. Blyth, A. S. B.	7935-40.
1 Calcutta	F. Stoliczka	8001.
1 Calcutta	J. Anderson	8942.
1 Calcutta (double headed)	No history	7985.
1 Calcutta	No history	13291.

1 Botanical Gardens, Calcutta	J. Anderson	8939.
12 Botanical Gardens, Calcutta	Purchased	8948-51, 8953-60.
2 Mutlah (Canning town)	W. Swinhoe	8929, 8935.
1 Suudarbans	W. Swinhoe	7978.
1 Silchar	O. L. Fraser	13273.
1 Dilcosh, N. E. Cachar	J. Inglis	11303.
2 Hailakandi, Cachar	C. H. Dreyer	4685-6.
2 Cachar	J. Anderson	8940-1.
1 Chittagong hill tracts	J. T. Jarbo	11414.
1 Akyab, Arakan	Dr. F. Day	7969.
1 Jergo Isle, Arakan	Marine Survey	12631.
2 Bhamo	Yunnan Exped. (J. Anderson)	7983, 7991.
2 Mandalay	Sir P. Sladen	7967.
1 Meiktalla, Burma	Genl. H. Collett	13252.
2 Proome	W. Dunn	7987-8.
5 Pegu	Major Berdmore, A. S. B.	7944-8.
1 Moulmein	Rev. F. Mason, A. S. B.	7949.
1 Semndaing, Tavoy	Museum Collector	12824.
1 Tavoy	Museum Collector	12711.
3 Mergui,	Mergui Exped. (J. Anderson)	11556-8.
2 Johore, Malay Peninsula	J. Meldrum	4657, 4661.
1 Andamans	Col. R. C. Tytler	8145.

(TYPE OF TYTLERIA HYPSIRHINOIDES, Theob.).

3 Andamans	Col. R. C. Tytler, A. S. B.	7942-3 8036.
1 Andamans	Capt. Hodge, A. S. B.	7941.
2 Andamans	Major Ford	7971, 7981.
1 Andamans	S. Kurtz	7591.
5 Andamans	J. Wood Mason	7992-6.
1 Andamans	Rev. J. Warneford	13238.
1 Nicobars	Museum Collector	7895.
2 Nicobars	F. Stoliczka	7979-80.
1 Nicobars	F. A. de Roepstorff.	8000.
2 "Mora"	Rev. H. J. Harrison	8525-6.
1 No loc.	Rev. H. J. Harrison	8665.
1 No loc.	No history, A. S. B.	7057.

75. LYCODON FASCIATUS, (Anders.).

Boulenger, p. 295; Sclater, J. A. S. B. lx, p. 234.
Distribution—Assam, Upper Burma and Yunan.

1 Shillong, Assam 4500 ft.	Major C. R. Cock	3853.
1 Tezpur, Assam	Duffla Exped. (Godwin Austen)	4003.

76. LYCODON GAMMIEI, (Blanf.).

Boulenger, p. 296.
Distribution—Sikkim.

1 Cinchona Pln., Darjeeling	J. A. Gammie	8447.

(TYPE OF THE SPECIES, Blanford.)

77. LYCODON SUBCINCTUS, Boie.

Günther, Rept. Brit. Ind., p. 322.
Distribution—Malay Peninsula, Java and Sumatra.

1 Singapore	Capt. Gardiner	13288.
2 Malay Peninsula	Raffles Mus. (W. Davison)	13321, 13327.

78. LYCODON EFFRENE, Cantor.

Günther, Rept. Brit. Ind., p. 320.
Distribution—Malay Peninsula, Banca and Borneo.

1 Banca Isl. Sumatra	Purchased	8004.

79. HYDROPHOBUS NYMPHA, (Daud.)

Boulenger, p. 298.
Distribution—South India and Ceylon.

4 No loc.	F. Stoliczka	3960-1, 4055, 8657.

80. HYDROPHOBUS DAVISONI, (Blanf.).

Boulenger, p. 299.
Distribution—Burma and Indo-China.

1 Nawlabu hill E. of Tavoy 1500 ft. (Davison)	W. T. Blanford	3201.
	(TYPE OF ULUPE DAVISONI, Blanford.)	
1 False Island, Arakan Coast?	Woodridge	8690.

81. HYDROPHOBUS SUBANNULATUS, (Dum. & Bibr.).

Günther, Rept. Brit. Ind., p. 235.
Distribution—Malay Peninsula and Sumatra.

1 Sinkip Isle N. of Sumatra	J. Wood Mason	8633.

82. PSEUDOCYCLOPHIS BICOLOR, (Bly.).

Boulenger, p. 300.
Distribution—Assam and Yunan.

1 Khasia hills	H. H. Godwin Austen	7032.
1 Charapunji	H. H. Godwin Austen	7037.
1 Assam	W. Robinson	7030.
	(TYPE OF THE SPECIES, Blyth).	
1 Muangla, Yunan	Yunan Exped. (J. Anderson)	4194.

83. PSEUDOCYCLOPHIS PERSICUS (Anders.)

Blanford, Persia, p. 408.
Distribution—Persia.

1 Bushire, Persia	Persian Collection (Mus. Coll.)	4828.

(TYPE OF THE SPECIES, Anderson.)

1 Niriz E. of Shiraz, Persia 5000 ft.	W. T. Blanford	3497.

84. POLYODONTOPHIS COLLARIS, (Gray).

Boulenger, p. 302.
Distribution—Himalayas from Simla eastwards, Assam, Burma, and S. China.

10 Darjeeling	J. A. Gammie	7169-70, 7183-7. 7740, 8809, 8821.
2 Darjeeling	W. S. Atkinson	7193, 7200.
1 Darjeeling	J. Anderson	7190.
1 Darjeeling	W. T. Blanford, A. S. B.	7239.

(TYPE OF COLUBER COLUBRINUS, Blyth ?)

1 Garo hills, Assam	H. H. Godwin Austen	7191.
1 Khasia hills	H. H. Godwin Austen	7202.
4 Charapunji	H. H. Godwin Austen	7188-9, 7195, 7197.
1 Jaintia hills	H. H. Godwin Austen	7192.
1 Hotha valley, Yunan	Yunan Exped. (Anderson)	4193.

85. POLYODONTOPHIS SUBPUNCTATUS (Dum. & Bibr.).

Boulenger, p. 303.
Distribution—Southern India and Ceylon.

1 Nr. Ellore, Godavery dist.	W. T. Blanford	7276.
1 Anamalai hills	Col. R. H. Beddome	4408.
1 Colombo	H. S. Ferguson	7275.
2 Bengal	No hist., A. S. B.	7073-4.

86. POLYODONTOPHIS SAGITTARIUS, (Cantor).

Boulenger, p. 303.
Distribution—Northern India, Bengal and the Nicobar Islands.

1 Gorakhpur dist., N. W. P.	A. C. L. Carlleyle	4684.
3 Darbhangah dist.	C. Maries	11926-8.
1 Manbhum	V. Ball	7068.
1 Serampore, Hugli dist.	C. R. S. Cadell	12095.
1 Maheshrekha, Hugli dist.	J. Wood Mason	8739.
1 Calcutta	O. L. Fraser	8722.
2 Botanical Gardens, Calcutta	J. Anderson	7067, 7069.
1 Camorta, Nicobars	F. A. de Roepstorff	8896.
1 "Bombay"	No history	8643.
3 Bengal	No history, A. S. B.	7071-2, 7075.
1 India	Rev. H. J. Harrison	8634.

87. POLYODONTOPHIS BISTRIGATUS, (Gunth.).

Boulenger, p. 304; Sclater, J. A. S. B. lx, p. 234.
Distribution—Burma and the Nicobar Islands.

1 Proome, Burma	Yunan Exped. (Anderson)	4200.
1 Comorta, Nicobars	F. A. de Roepstorff	8901.

88. POLYODONTOPHIS MELANOCEPHALUS, (Gray).

Günther, Rept. Brit. Ind., p. 229.
Distribution—Malay Peninsula.

2 Singapore	Capt. T. S. Gardiner	12811, 13283.
1 Singapore	Purchased	7203.

89. ABLABES CALAMARIA, (Gunth.).

Boulenger, p. 305.
Distribution—Indian Peninsula and Ceylon.

1 Sirguja, Chota Nagpur	V. Ball	7204.
1 Tinnevelli hills	Col. R. H. Beddome	4421.
2 Madras Pr.	Col. R. H. Beddome	8734-5.
1 South India	E. Gerard [P.]	12371.

90. ABLABES STOLICZKAE, Scl.

Sclater, J. A. S. B. lx, p. 234, pl. vi, fig. 1
Distribution—Assam.

1 Samaguting, Assam	Capt. J. Butler	8725.
1 No loc.	F. Stoliczka	3955.

(CO-TYPES OF THE SPECIES, SCL.)

91. ABLABES SCRIPTUS, Theob.

Boulenger, p. 305.
Distribution—Burma.

1 Martaban, Burma	Major Berdmore, A. S. B.	7207.

(TYPE OF THE SPECIES, Theobald.)

92. ABLABES FRENATUS (Gunth.).

Boulenger, p. 306.
Distribution—Assam.

1 Assam	W. Robinson, A. S. B.	8029.

93. ABLABES DORIAE, (Boul.).

Boulenger, p. 306; Sclater, J. A. S. B. lx, p. 235.
Distribution—Kakhyen hills and Manipur.

1 Manipur	R. D. Oldham	11939.

94. ABLABES RAPPII, Gunth.

Boulenger, p. 307.
Distribution—Himalayas from Simla to Darjeeling.

1 Simla	F. Stoliczka	8370.
8 Darjeeling	J. A. Gammie	7171, 7173-8, 7739.
1 Lingling, Kurseong	J. Johnstone	8439.
1 Mongpoo, Kurseong	J. L. Lister	8699.

95. ABLABES NICOBARIENSIS, Stol.

Boulenger, p. 307.
Distribution—Nicobars.

1 Camorta, Nicobars	F. Stoliczka [P.]	7201.

(TYPE OF THE SPECIES, Stoliczka.)

96. ABLABES PORPHYRACEUS, (Cantor).

Boulenger, p. 308.
Distribution—Sikkim, Assam, Burma, Yunan and Sumatra.

19 Darjeeling	J. A. Gammie.	7216-7, 7219-20. 7222-5, 7231-3, 7728-9. 8478-9, 8796-8, 8804-5.
1 Darjeeling	Capt. Jerdan	7236.
1 Darjeeling	W. S. Atkinson	7227.
1 Darjeeling	J. Anderson	7228.
1 Nagaisuree, Jalpi. dist.	G. W. Shillingford	12668.
1 Terai Ghat	H. J. Elwes	13088.
1 Garo hills, Assam	Capt. Williamson	3943.
2 Charapunji	Lt. J. H. Bourne	7229-30.
1 Samagnting	Capt. J. Butler	7235.
2 Sibsagar, Assam	S. E. Peal	7221, 7226.
2 Momien, Yunnan	Yunan Exped. (Anderson)	4197-8.
1 Hotha, Kakhyen hills	Yunan Exped. (Anderson)	4184.
1 Pwehla, Shan States, 4000 ft.	General Collett	13194.
1 No loc.	Col. H. H. Godwin Austen	7237.

97. ABLABES MODESTUS, Martin.

Blanford, Persia, p. 403.
Distribution—Persia, Asia Minor and Transcaucasia.

1 Karij valley, Elbruz, Persia 6000 ft.	Persian Coll. (Blanford)	8455.
1 Kohrnd, N. of Ispahan 8000 ft.	Persian Coll. (Blanford)	8456.

98. ABLABES COLLARIS, (Menetries).

Blanford, Persia, p. 405.
Distribution—Persia, Asia Minor and Transcaucasia.

2 Betw. Khan Jubb Yusef and Ain Mella beg, Gallilee	J. Anderson	11112, 11114.

99. ABLABES FASCIATUS, (Jan).

Blanford, Persia, p. 406.
Distribution—Persia and Palestine.

1 Dehgirdu betw. Shiraz and Ispahan	Persian Coll. (Blanford)	3490.

100. ABLABES TRICOLOR, (Schleg.).

Stoliczka, J. A. S. B. xlii, p. 122.
Distribution—Sumatra, Java and Borneo.

2 Dehli, Sumatra	L. Schwendler	11448, 11450.
1 No loc.	No hist.	8704.

101. CORONELLA BRACHYURA, (Gunth.).

Boulenger, p. 309.
Distribution—Peninsula of India.

1 Poona dist.	G. Vidal	11410.
1 Wun, S. E. Berar	W. T. Blanford	7335.

102. CORONELLA DECORATA, (Gunth.).

Günther, Cat. Col. Snakes, p. 35.
Distribution—Mexico and West Indies.

1 West Indies	Netley Mus. [Ex.]	8676.

103. CORONELLA CANA (Linn.).

Gunther, Cat. Col. Snakes, p. 40.
Distribution—South Africa.

1 Cape of Good Hope	Netley Mus. [Ex.]	8639.
1 S. Africa	Purchased	7590.

(TYPE OF CADMUS CUNEIFORMIS, Theobald.)

104. CORONELLA PHOCARUM, Gunth.

Günther, P. Z. S. 1872, p. 836.
Distribution—Robben Island, Cape Colony.

1 Robben Isl. Cape Colony	E. Gerard [P.]	12403.

105. LIOPHIS COBELLA, (Linn.).

Gunther, Cat. Col. Snakes, p. 43.
Distribution—Tropical parts of South America.

2 Demarara	D. Carruthers	3197-8.
1 Bahia, Brazil	E. Gerard [P.]	12358.
1 Tropical America	Netley Mus. [Ex.]	8651.

106. LIOPHIS MERREMII, (Neuwied).

Günther, Cat. Col. Snakes, p. 44.
Distribution—Tropical South America.

1 "South America"	British Mus. [Ex.]	4745.

107. LIOPHIS REGINAE, (Linn.).

Günther, Cat. Col. Snakes, p. 46.
Distribution—South America and West Indies ?

1 West Indies	G. E. Dobson	8431.

108. DIADOPHIS PUNCTATUS, (Linn.).

Garman, Snakes N. America, p. 72.
Distribution—Eastern States and Canada.

1 Ontario, Canada.	Dr. J. H. Garnier, [Ex.]	12222.

109. OPHIBOLUS TRIANGULIGERUS, (Boie).

Garman, Snakes N. America, p. 65.
Distribution—Canada and the States.

1 Lake Erie, Canada	Dr. J. H. Garnier, [Ex.]	12270.
2 Lake Scanlanou, Ontario, Canada	Dr. J. H. Garnier, [Ex.]	12169-70.
2 Ontario, Canada	Dr. J. H. Garnier, [Ex.]	12112, 12229.
2 Texas, U. S. A.	Dr. J. H. Garnier, [Ex.]	12268-9.
1 Chehnahna, Mexico	Dr. J. H. Garnier, [Ex.]	12273.

110. OPHIBOLUS GETULUS, (Linn.).

Garman, Snakes N. America, p. 68.
Distribution—South Eastern States of North America.

2 N. Carolina	Rev. F. Fitzgerald, A. S. B.	7213-4.

111. RHINOCHEILUS LECONTEI, Baird and Girard.

Garman, Snakes N. America, p. 73.
Distribution—South California and Mexico.

1 Texas	Dr. J. H. Garnier [Ex.]	12246.

112. CYCLOPHIS VERNALIS, (Harlan).

Garman, Snakes N. America, p. 39.
Distribution—N. America, east of the Rocky Mountains.

2 Ontario, Canada	Dr. J. H. Garnier, [Ex.]	12156, 12206.

113. CYCLOPHIS AESTIVUS, (Linn.).

Garman, Snakes N. America, p. 40.
Distribution—Eastern United States.

2 N. Carolina, U. S. A.	Rev. F. Fitzgerald, A. S. B.	7209-10.
1 Texas, U. S. A.	Dr. J. H. Garnier, [Ex.]	12209.

114. HETERODON PLATYRHINUS, Latr.

Garman, Snakes N. America, p. 75.
Distribution—Eastern United States and Canada.

1 St. Clair Flats, Ontario, Canada	Dr. J. H. Garnier, [Ex.]	12165.
1 Texas, U. S. A.	Dr. J. H. Garnier, [Ex.]	12158.

115. HETERODON DORBIGNII, Dum. & Bibr.

Günther, Cat. Col. Snakes, p. 83.
Distribution—Southern part of South America.

1 Montevideo, Uraguay	British Mus. [Ex.]	4749.
1 Buenos Ayres	E. Gerard [P.]	12405.

116. DROMICUS LINEATUS, (Linn.).

Günther, Cat. Col. Snakes, p. 134.
Distribution—Tropical South America.

1 "S. America"	E. Gerard [P.]	12368.

117. SIMOTES CYCLURUS, (Cantor).

Boulenger, p. 311; Sclater, J. A. S. B. lx, p. 235.
Distribution—Bengal, Assam, Burma, Indo- and South China.

1 Caragola, Purneah Dist.	T. S. Hill	12356.
2 Calcutta	Purchased	7094-5.
3 Kaliganj Rungpur Dist.	W. Dodgson	7085, 7087-8.
3 Darjeeling ?	Dr. G. King	8611-13.
1 Nagasurie, Jalpi. dist.	G. W. Shillingford	12878.
2 Garo hills, Assam	Capt. Williamson	3940, 7089.
1 Rangoon	Mergui Exped. (J. Anderson)	11571.
4 Pegu	W. Theobald	7091-2, 7097, 7099.
1 Pegu	E. Gerard [P.]	12390.
1 Moulmein Dist.	Capt. Hood	7093.
1 Tavoy	Museum Coll.	12712.
1 Tenasserim	Tenass. Exped. (Limborg.)	8616.
1 No loc.	No hist.	7163.

(TYPE OF S. CRASSUS, Theobald.)

2 No loc.	No hist.	7126-7.

(TYPES OF S. OBSCURUS, Theobald.)

2 No loc.	No hist., A. S. B.	7096, 7105.
4 No loc.	No hist.	7000, 7098, 8075, 8569.

118. SIMOTES ALBOCINCTUS, (Cantor).

Boulenger, p. 312.
Distribution—Sikkim, Assam, the Chittagong and Arakan hills.

1 Jellapahar, Darjeeling 7,500 ft.	R. D'Cruz.	12842.
17 Darjeeling	J. Gammie	7132-4, 7137-40, 7141 7152, 7160, 7206, 7730 7743-4, 8471, 8808, 8811.
4 Darjeeling	Capt. Jerdan	7135-6, 7155, 7205.
1 Darjeeling	J. Anderson	7146.
1 N. E. Himalayas	J. Cockburn	8680.
1 Kaliganj, Rungpur dist.	W. Dodgson	7086.
1 Buxa, Doars	Museum Coll.	12563.
1 Goalpara, Assam	H. L. Haughton	7145.
2 Garo hills	Capt. Williamson	3938, 3939.
1 Khasia hills	W. Atkinson	7159.
2 Charapunji	Col. H. H. Godwin Austen	7156, 7158.
2 Jaintia hills	Col. H. H. Godwin Austen	7142-3.
5 Samaguting	Capt. J. Butler	7124, 7149-51, 7165.
5 Sibsagar	S. E. Peal	4027, 4037-40.
2 Assam	W. Robinson, A. S. B.	7106, 7108.
1 Dilcosh, N. E. Cachar	J. Inglis	11360.
2 Cachar	Museum Coll. (Sheik Hurri)	7147-8.
2 Chittagong	B. Macdonald	7889-90.
1 Chittagong	C. A. Mills	13192.

119. SIMOTES PURPURASCENS, (Schleg.).

Boulenger, P. Z. S. 1890, p. 34; Sclater, J. A. S. B. lx, p. 235.
Distribution—Tenasserim, Malay Peninsula, Sumatra and Borneo.

1 Tavoy	Mergui Exped. (Anderson)	11565.
1 Penang	F. Stoliczka	8378.
1 Johore	J. Wood Mason	7513.
	(2 Types of S. catenifer, Stoliczka.)	
2 Singapore	Raffles Mus. (Davison)	13307-8.

120. SIMOTES VIOLACEUS, (Cantor).

Boulenger, p. 312.
Distribution—Assam, Tenasserim, Cambodia and South China.

1 Charapunji, Khasia hills.	Col. H. H. Godwin Austen	7157.
2 Naga hills	Capt. Gregory	7167-8.
	(Type of Simotes semifasciatus, Anders.)	
3 Samaguting, Assam	Capt. J. Butler	7161-2, 7164.
1 Nazira, Assam	J. Foster	7166.
1 Assam	W. Robinson, A. S. B.	7107.
1 Manipur	R. D. Oldham	11938.
1 Chittagong hills.	J. T. Jarbo	11412.

121. SIMOTES WOODMASONI, Scl.

Sclater, J. A. S. B. lx, p. 235.

Distribution—Andaman and Nicobar Islands.

1 Andamans	J. Wood Mason	8459.
1 Nicobars	F. A. de Roepstorff	12547.

(CO-TYPES OF THE SPECIES SCL.)

122. SIMOTES OCTOLINEATUS, (Schneid.).

Boulenger, p. 313.

Distribution—South India, Malay Peninsula, Sumatra, Borneo and Java.

1 Singapore	Derrick Spon	12967.
3 Singapore	Capt. T. S. Gardiner	12638-9, 12806.
1 Singapore ?	Raffles Museum	13310.
1 Deli, Sumatra	Capt. T. S. Gardiner	12845.

123. SIMOTES ARNENSIS, (Shaw).

Boulenger, p. 314.

Distribution—The Himalayas and thoughout India to Ceylon extending eastwards to Rungpur in Bengal.

1 Almora, N. W. Himalayas	A. W. Lawder	4129.
1 Allahabad	J. Cockburn	8679.
1 Nowgong, C. P.	F. J. Daley	13414.
1 Colombo, Ceylon	W. Ferguson	7120.
2 Aska, Ganjam dist.	E. A. Minchin	12946-7.
1 Singbhum	V. Ball	7117.
1 Serampore, Hugli dist.	Gen. G. B. Mainwaring	12634.
1 Calcutta	Sir J. Fayrer	7118.
1 Alipore near Calcutta	Sir J. Fayrer	7123.
1 Ballygunj, " "	Sir J. Fayrer	7121.
2 Kaliganj, Rungpur dist.	W. Dodgson	7109-10.
1 No loc.	A. Grote	7116.
1 No loc.	Col. R. H. Beddome	4427.

124. SIMOTES THEOBALDI, Gunth.

Boulenger, p. 315; Sclater, J. A. S. B. lx, p. 236.

Distribution—Burma, from Mandalay to Mergui.

1 Mandalay, Burma	Yunan Exped. (J. Anderson)	4199.
2 Meiktalla, Burma	General Collett	13236-7.
1 Mergui	No history, A. S. B.	7104.

125. SIMOTES CRUENTATUS, Gunth.

Boulenger, p. 315.

Distribution—The Pegu division of Burma.

1 Rangoon	W. Theobald, A. S. B.	7130.
2 Pegu	F. Stoliczka	8361, 8369.

126. SIMOTES PLANICEPS, Boul.

Boulenger, p. 316, Sclater, J. A. S. B. lx, p. 236.
Distribution—Burma.

1 No loc.	Yunan Exped. (Anderson)	4154.

127. SIMOTES SIGNATUS, Gunth.

Günther, Rept. Brit. Ind., p. 215.
Distribution—Malay Peninsula.

1 Singapore	Raffles Mus. (Davison)	13309.

128. OLIGODON AFFINIS, Gunth.

Boulenger, p. 318.
Distribution—Anamalai and Travancore hills.

1 Malabar	Col. R. H. Beddome	4422.
1 Travancore hills	Col. R. H. Beddome	4426.

129. OLIGODON DORSALIS, (Gray).

Boulenger, p. 319; Sclater, J. A. S. B. lx, p. 237.
Distribution—Assam and Chittagong hills.

1 Garo hills	Capt. Williamson	3944.
1 Khasia hills	N. Belletty	7081.
1 Samaguting	Capt. J. Butler	7082.
1 Chittagong	Mrs. Bruce	2881.

130. OLIGODON SUBLINEATUS, Dum. & Bibr.

Boulenger, p. 320; Sclater, J. A. S. B. lx, p. 237.
Distribution—Ceylon and the Nicobars.

1 Columbo, Ceylon	W. Ferguson	7080.
1 Ceylon	Col. R. H. Beddome	4406.
4 Ceylon	H. Nevill	8671-4.
1 Ceylon	J. Anderson	4809.
2 Camorta, Nicobars	F. A. de Roepstorff	8899-8900.
1 No loc.	Col. R. H. Beddome	8389.

131. OLIGODON SUBGRISEUS, Dum. & Bibr.

Boulenger, p. 321; Sclater, J. A. S. B. lx, p. 237.
Distribution—Throughout India and Ceylon extending from British Beluchistan to Purneah in Bengal.

1 Killa Abdulla nr. Khojak, Brit. Baluchistan	J. A. Murray	11423.
1 Karachi	Karachi Mus. [Ex.]	7079.
2 Sind	J. A. Murray	11711, 12012.
1 Rajanpur, Pjb.	D. D. Cunningham	8594.
1 Rajanpur, Pjb.	Dr. E. Sanders	8380.
1 Dehra, N. W. P.	Col. J. Biddulph	8693.

1 Upper Godavery dist., C. P.	Dr. Goffney	7070.
3 Malabar	Col. R. H. Beddome	8381-3.
2 Anamalai hills	Col. R. H. Beddome	4402, 4405.
3 Tinnevelli hills	Col. R. H. Beddome	4403, 4417, 4428.
1 Travancore	Col. R. H. Beddome	4415.
2 South India	E. Gerard [P.]	12357, 60.
4 Ceylon	E. L. Layard, A. S. B.	7100-3.
1 Chota Nagpur	V. Ball	7078.
1 Caragola, Purneah dist.	T. S. Hill	12553.
2 Domercoonda (Barrakur)	F. S. Buchanan	7076-7.
1 No loc.	Col. R. H. Beddome	4378.
1 No loc.	No hist.	8702.

132. OLIGODON MELANOCEPHALUS, (Gunth.).

Boulenger, p. 317; Sclater, J. A. S. B. lx, p. 237.
Distribution—Western Asia, from Syria to Sinai.

2 Samaria, Palestine	J. Anderson	11241-2.

133. RHAGERRHIS PRODUCTA, (Gerv.).

Sclater, J. A. S. B. lx, p. 237.
Distribution—North Africa extending eastwards to Persia.

1 Tanjistan, Persia	J. A. Murray	12000.

134. PSAMMOPHYLAX RHOMBEATUS, (Linn.).

Günther, Cat. Col. Snakes, p. 31.
Distribution— South and West Africa.

1 Accra W. Africa	Berlin Mus. [Ex.]	7913.
1 No loc.	No history.	8669.

135. ZAMENIS KORROS, (Schleg.).

Boulenger, p. 324; Sclater, J. A. S. B. lx, p. 237.
Distribution—Ceylon ?, Assam, Burma, South China, Siam, Malay Peninsula, Sumatra and Java.

1 Ceylon ?	E. F. Kelaart, A. S. B.	7295.
1 Nazira, Assam	J. M. Foster	7299.
1 Silchar	O. L. Fraser	13273.
2 Chittagong	B. Macdonald	7881-2.
1 Rangoon	Sir J. Fayrer, A. S. B.	7297.
1 Hotha, Yunan	Yunan Exped. (Anderson)	7300.
1 Sanda valley, Yunan	Yunan Exped. (Anderson)	7298.
1 Moulmein	Capt. Hood	7413.
1 Mergui	Mergui Exped. (Anderson)	11569.
1 Tenasserim	Tenasserim Exped. (Limborg)	6848.

136. ZAMENIS MUCOSUS, (Linn.).

Boulenger, p. 324.
Distribution—Afghanistan and Beluchistan, Himalayas, India

and Ceylon, Assam, Burma, Andamans, South China, Siam, Malay Peninsula and Java.

1 Quetta	Sir O. B. C. St. John	11691.
1 Chitral	G. M. Giles	13080.
2 Kashmir	Yarkand Exped. (Stoliczka)	8460-1.
2 Kashmir	G. W. Strettel	12600-1.
1 Kotgarh, Simla	F. Stoliczka	7286.
1 Subathu nr. Simla	Rev. Cave Brown, A. S. B.	7279.
1 Almora, Kumaon	A. W. Lawder	4130.
1 Rajanpur, Pjb.	Dr. E. Sanders	7292.
1 Ajmere, Rjpt.	Sir O. B. C. St. John	13480.
1 Nagpore	Mus. Collector	7294.
1 Travancore	Trevandrum Mus.	13505.
1 Chandbally, Orissa	C. H. Dreyer	12570.
1 Chandernagore	J. F. Galiffe	8427.
1 Kaliganj, Rungpur dist.	W. Dodgson	7291.
2 Goalpara, Assam	Dr. Thorburn, A. S. B.	7280-1.
1 Momien, Yunan	Yunan Exped. (Anderson)	7290.
1 Mandalay	" " "	7288.
2 Port Blair, Andamans	Col. Tytler	7278, 7282.
1 Andamans	G. E. Dobson	7289.
1 India	E. Gerard [P.]	12404.

137. ZAMENIS VENTRIMACULATUS, (Gray).

Boulenger, p. 325; Sclater, J. A. S. B. lx, p. 238.

Distribution—North West Himalayas, Northern and Western India.

1 Bushire ?	Karachi Mus. [Ex.]	8400.
1 Below Simla	F. Stoliczka [P.]	7265.
1 Subathu nr. Simla	The Rev. Cave Brown	7240.

(Type of Platyceps semifasciatus, Bly.).

1 Rajanpur, Pjb.	Dr. D. D. Cunningham	8592.
1 Jeypore, Rjpt.	R. Pattoon, [Ex.]	8437.
1 Rajpootana	N. Belletty	13385.
6 Karachi	Karachi Mus. [Ex.]	7313, 7320, 8399, 8606, 8664, 8748.
4 No loc.	No hist., A. S. B.	7304-7.

138. ZAMENIS LADACCENSIS, Anders.

Boulenger, p. 326; Sclater, J. A. S. B. lx, p. 238.

Distribution—Egypt and Arabia extending eastwards through Persia, Afghanistan and Beluchistan to Ladak.

2 Shiraz	Persian Coll. (Mus. Coll.)	7676-7.

(Types of Gonyosoma dorsalis, Anders.).

3 Shiraz	Persian Coll. (Mus. Coll.)	7336-7, 4827.
2 Bushire	Karachi Mus. [Ex.]	8401-2.
5 Bushire	W. D. Cumming.	13423-4, 13416-8.
1 Karman, S. E. Persia	Persian Coll. (Blanford)	4615.
1 Regan, S. E. Persia	Persian Coll. (Blanford)	8601.
1 South Persia	Persian Coll. (Blanford)	8602.
1 Askan, Baluch.	Persian Coll. (Blanford)	4618.
2 Zamran, Baluch.	Persian Coll. (Blanford)	4616, 8603.

1 Hung, Baluch.	Persian Coll. (Blanford)	3494.
2 Quetta	Sir O. B. C. St. John	11695-6.
1 Gilgit dist.	Col. J. Biddulph	8605.
1 Kula, Ladak	Dr. Cayley	7323.
	(TYPE OF THE SPECIES ANDERSON).	
1 Ladak	No history	7274.

139. ZAMENIS KARELINI, (Brandt).

Boulenger, p. 326.

Distribution—Persia, Afghanistan, Beluchistan and Turkestan.

1 Chinkilok, nr. Herat	Afghan Bound. Comm.	13107.
1 Quetta, Bt. Beluch.	Sir O. B. C. St. John.	11694.

140. ZAMENIS FASCIOLATUS, (Shaw).

Boulenger, p. 327.

Distribution—Throughout India ; Wellesley Prov. in Malay peninsula ?

3 Allahabad	J. Cockburn	8570-2.
1 Collagelly hills Coimb. dist.	Col. R. H. Beddome	8469.
1 Anamalai hills	Col. R. H. Beddome	4379.
1 South India	Dr. T. C. Jerdon, A. S. B.	7333.
1 South India	E. Gerard [P]	12374.
1 Monghyr	J. Lockwood	8713.
1 Calcutta	Sir J. Fayrer, A. S. B.	7332.
1 Near Calcutta	J. F. Galiffe	7334.
1 No loc.	F. Stoliczka	8659.

141. ZAMENIS DIADEMA, (Shaw).

Boulenger, p. 327 ; Sclater, J. A. S. B. lx, p. 238.

Distribution—From Algeria eastwards throughout Western Asia to the North West Provinces of India and northward to Turkestan.

2 Ispahan	Persian Coll. (Mus. Coll.)	7314-5.
3 Karman, S. E. Persia	Persian Coll. (Blanford)	3489, 8589, 4617.
2 South Persia	Persian Coll. (Blanford)	3492-3.
1 E. of Bampur, Beluch.	Persian Coll. (Blanford)	8588.
1 Dizak, Beluch.	Persian Coll. (Blanford)	8590.
1 Kaghul, Chitral, 5,500 ft.	G. M. Giles	12882.
1 Chitral	G. M. Giles	13161.
1 Gilgit	Col. Biddulph	8604.
2 Rajanpur, Punjab.	Dr. E. Sanders	7321, 8738.
1 Rajanpur, Punjab.	Dr. D. D. Cunningham	8591.
1 Lahore	J. A. Murray	11999
2 Delhi	J. Anderson	7308-9
1 Punjab	Sir J. Fayrer	7319.
3 Jeypore, Rajputana	R. Pattoon, [Ex.]	7310, 7316, 7322.
3 Agra, N. W. P.	Agra Mus. [Ex.]	7311-2, 7318.
1 Allahabad	J. Cockburn.	8712.
1 Near Bhartpur, C. I.	Agra Mus. [Ex.]	7317.
1 Purneah ?	Purchased	10978.
1 India	Rev. H. J. Harrison	8552.
1 No loc.	Netley Mus. [Ex.]	8443.
1 No loc.	F. Stoliczka	3886.

142. ZAMENIS ARENARIUS, Boul.

Boulenger, p. 329.
Distribution—Rajpootana and Sind.

1 Rajpootana	N. Belletty.	13383.

143. ZAMENIS RAVERGIERI, (Menetries).

Blanford, Persia, p. 417.
Distribution—Palestine, Transcaucasia, Persia and Eastern Turkestan.

1 Kohrud, N. of Ispahan	Persian Coll. (Blanford)	4610.
4 Near Shiraz	Persian Coll. (Blanford)	7328-31
1 Kaman, Shiraz Road	Persian Coll. (Blanford)	8587.
1 Karman, S. E. Persia	Persian Coll. (Blanford)	4609.
1 S. Persia	Persian Coll. (Blanford)	8586.
1 Yarkand	Yarkand Exped. (Stoliczka)	8677.
2 Yangihissar	Yarkand Exped. (Stoliczka)	8607-8
2 Eastern Turkestan	J. Scully	13197-8.

144. ZAMENIS DAHLII, Dum. & Bibr.

Blanford, Persia, p. 417.
Distribution—South-eastern Europe, North-eastern Africa, Asia Minor, Transcaucasia and Persia.

1 Galilee, Palestine	J. Anderson	11033.

145. ZAMENIS HIPPOCREPIS, (Merr.).

Schreiber, Herp. Europ., p. 260.
Distribution—Southern Europe from Spain to Greece.

1 Germany	E. Gerard [P.]	12387.
1 South Europe	Brit. Mus. [Ex.]	4744.
1 Mediterranean Region	Netley Mus. [Ex.]	8545.

146. ZAOCCYS NIGROMARGINATUS, (Bly.)

Boulenger, p. 329.
Distribution—Sikkim, Assam and Kakhyen hills of Upper Burma.

1 Darjeeling	W. Sherwill, A. S. B.	7343.
	(TYPE OF THE SPECIES, Blyth.)	
3 Darjeeling	J. Gammie	8807, 8819, 8827.
1 Darjeeling	J. Anderson	7338.
1 Darjeeling	W. S. Atkinson	7340.
1 Rungbee, Darjeeling dist.	Dr. G. King	8610.
3 Sikkim	No history, A. S. B.	7344-6.
1 Khasia hills	Col. H. H. Godwin Austen	7347.
1 Charapunji	Col. H. H. Godwin Austen	7342.
1 Cherapunji	J. H. Bourne	7348.

147. ZAOCCYS TENASSERIMENSIS, (Scl.).

Sclater, J. A. S. B., xl, p. 238.
Distribution—Tenasserim.

1 Tenasserim — Tenasserim Expd. (Limborg) — 4073.

(TYPE OF THE SPECIES, Sclater.)

148. ZAOCCYS FUSCUS, (Gunth.).

Günther, Cat. Col. Snakes, p. 112.
Distribution—Malay Peninsula and Borneo.

1 Singapore — Raffles Mus. (Davison) — 13313.

149. SALVADORA GRAHAMIAE, (Baird and Girard).

Garman, N. Amer. Snakes, p. 38.
Distribution—Southern United States and Mexico.

1 Texas — Dr. J. H. Garnier, [Ex.] — 12186.

150. HERPETODRYAS CARINATUS, (Linn.).

Günther, Cat. Col. Snakes, p. 115.
Distribution—Tropical parts of South America and Central America.

1 Costa Rica — E. Gerard [P.]. — 12384.

151. HERPETODRYAS BODDAERTI, (Seezen).

Günther, Cat. Col. Snakes, p. 115.
Distribution—Tropical parts of South America.

1 Demerara — D. Carruthers — 3195.

152. HERPETODRYAS BERNIERI, (Dum. & Bibr.).

Dum. et Bibr. Erpet. Gen., vii, p. 211.
Distribution—Madagascar.

1 Marovare, Madagascar — Purchased — 11471.

153. PITYOPHIS MELANOLEUCUS, (Daud.).

Garman, N. Amer. Snakes, p. 51.
Distribution—Eastern United States.

2 Elk. R. Minnesota, U. S. A. — Dr. J. H. Garnier [Ex.] — 12757-8.

154. PITYOPHIS CATENIFER (Blainv.).

Garman, N. Amer. Snakes, p. 52.
Distribution—Southern and Western United States.

1 Espontoso, Texas U. S. A. — Dr. J. H. Garnier [Ex.] — 12756.
1 Texas — Dr. J. H. Garnier [Ex.] — 12232.

155. COLUBER HELENA, (Daud.).

Boulenger, p. 331 ; Sclater, J. A. S. B. lx, p. 239.

Distribution—Throughout India and Ceylon extending to Assam.

1 Karachi	Karachi Mus. [Ex.]	8719.
1 Ajmere, Rajpootana	Sir O. B. C. St. John	13477.
7 Jeypore, Rajpootana	R. Pattocn	8547-51, 8561-2
1 Mt. Aboo, Rajpootana	G. S. Sutherland	7269.
1 Shevaroy hills, Salem dist.	B. Daly	13525.
1 Madamally, Malabar dist.	Col. R. H. Beddome	7572.
1 Madras Pr.	Col. R. H. Beddome	7271.
1 South India	Dr. T. C. Jerdon, A. S. B.	7266.
1 20 m. W. of Galle, Ceylon	J. Anderson	7270.
1 Ceylon	E. Gerard [P.]	12396.
1 Caragola, Purneah dist.	T. S. Hill	12554.
1 Mutlah, 24-Parganas	W. Swinhoe	7035.
1 Samaguting, Assam	Capt. J. Butler	8882.
2 No loc.	Col. R. H. Beddome	8384-5.
1 No loc.	E. Gerard [P.]	12397.
1 No loc.	No hist., A. S. B.	7267.
2 No loc.	No hist., A. S. B.	7272-3.

156. COLUBER RETICULARIS, (Cantor).

Boulenger, p. 332 ; Sclater, J. A. S. B., lx, p. 239.

Distribution—Sikkim, Assam and Burma.

7 Darjeeling	J. A. Gammie	7250-1, 7255-6, 7258, 8482, 8810.
1 Darjeeling	Capt. Jerdan	7260.
1 Rungbee, Darjeeling	Dr. G. King	8711.
2 Gompahar, Darjeeling 7,500 ft.	J. S. Gamble	12020-1.
1 Dhobyhora, Kurseong 6000 ft.	J. S. Gamble	12019.
1 Garo hills, Assam	N. Belletty	7245.
1 Ramri isle, Arakan	Purchased, A. S. B.	7327.
2 Pegu	A. S. B.	7325-6.
1 No loc.	No hist, A. S. B.	7324.

157. COLUBER HODGSONII, (Gunth.)

Boulenger, p. 332.

Distribution—The Himalayas, from Ladak to Sikkim.

1 Kashmir	No hist.	8436.
3 Simla	Purchased	7261-3.
3 Katmandu, Nepal	Museum Collector	7252-4.

158. COLUBER TAENIURUS, (Cope)

Boulenger, p. 333 ; Sclater, J. A. S. B. lx, p. 239.

Distribution—Sikkim, Burma, Manchuria, China, Indo-China, Borneo and Sumatra.

1 Cinchona Pln., Darjeeling	J. Lister	8412.
3 Momien, Yunan	Yunan Exped. (Anderson)	4180-2.

(TYPES OF ELAPHIS YUNNANENSIS, Anderson).

1 Burma	Col. Nuthall, A. S. B.	7238.
	(TYPE OF C. NUTHALLI, Theobald).	
1 Shanghai	British Mus. [Ex.]	4742.

159. COLUBER RADIATUS, (Schleg.).

Boulenger, p. 333; Sclater, J. A. S. B. lx, p. 239.

Distribution—Bengal, Sikkim, Assam, Burma, Malay Peninsula, China, Indo-China, Java and Sumatra.

1 Backergunj, Bengal	E. Taylor	7248.
2 Samaguting, Assam	Capt. J. Butler	8873, 7264.
1 Sibsagar	S. E. Peal	4010.
1 Cachar	O. L. Fraser	13282.
2 Chittagong	B. Macdonald	7888, 7891.
1 Chittagong hill tracts	J. T. Jarbo	11411.
3 Ramri Isle, Arakan	Capt. Abbott, A. S. B.	7241-3.
1 Mandalay	Yunan Expd. (Anderson)	4183.
1 Mandalay	F. B. Sladen	8694.
1 Pegu	E. Gerard [P.]	12381.
1 Nr. Assoon, Moulmein dist.	Tenasserim Exped. (Limborg)	8752.
1 Amiah, Tavoy dist.	Museum Collector	12817.
3 Mergui	Mergui Exped. (Anderson)	11584-5; 11564.
1 Johore, Malay P.	J. Meldrum	4654.
1 Hongkong	Hongkong Mus. [Ex.]	12697.
1 Hongkong	Dr. Hungerford	13172.
1 No loc.	No hist., A. S. B.	7259.
1 No loc.	F. Stoliczka	8367.

160. COLUBER MELANURUS, (Schleg.).

Boulenger, p. 334.

Distribution—Tenasserim, Andamans, Malay Peninsula, Sumatra, Borneo, Java and Celebes.

2 Andaman Isles	Major Ford	7244-6.
1 Andaman Isles	Purchased	7247.
1 Elphistone Isle, Mergui	Dr. J. Anderson	11559.
1 Kwala Lumpore, Malay Peninsula	Raffles Mus. (Davison)	13311.
1 Dehli, Sumatra	L. Schwendler	11439.
1 Borneo	E. Gerard [P.]	12378.

161. COLUBER PRASINUS, Bly.

Boulenger, p. 334; Sclater, J. A. S. B. lx, p. 239.

Distribution—Sikkim, Assam and Upper Burma.

2 Darjeeling	J. Gammie	7733, 7927.
2 Garo hills, Assam	Capt. Williamson	3937, 8486.
2 Samaguting	Capt. J. Butler	7674-5.
3 Assam	W. Robinson, A. S. B.	7669-71.
	(TYPES OF THE SPECIES, Blyth.).	
1 Bhamo	Yunan Exped. (Anderson)	4201.

162. COLUBER OXYCEPHALUS, Boie.

Boulenger, p. 335; Sclater, J. A. S. B. lx, p. 239.
Distribution—Sikkim, Burma, Andamans, Nicobars, Malay Peninsula and Islands.

1 Darjeeling	J. Gammie	8483.
1 Pegu	Major Berdmore, A. S. B.	7668.
1 Mergui	W. Theobald, A. S. B.	7667.
1 Andamans	Capt. Hodge, A. S. B	7666.
1 Andamans	Capt. Homfray, A. S. B.	7679.
1 Andamans	W. Theobald	7678.
2 Andamans	Col. Tytler	7672-3.
1 Perak	Mus. Coll. (Jaffa)	13249.
1 Singapore	Raffles Mus. (Davison)	13317.
1 Labuan, Borneo	Hongkong Mus. [Ex.]	12689.

163. COLUBER SUBRADIATUS, (Schleg.).

Günther, Cat. Col. Snakes, p. 95.
Distribution—The Philippine Islands.

1 Philippines	Hongkong Mus. [Ex.]	12688.

164. COLUBER ESCULAPII, (Boie).

Schreiber, Herp. Europ., p. 281.
Distribution—Southern Europe from Spain to Turkey.

1 South Europe	G. A. Boulenger	13029.

165. COLUBER CONSTRICTOR, Linn.

Garman, N. Amer. Snakes, p. 41.
Distribution—Eastern half of the United States.

2 Massachusetts, U. S. A.	Dr. J. H. Garnier [Ex.]	12228, 12764.
1 South Carolina, U. S. A.	Rev. F. Fitzgerald, A. S. B.	7301.
1 Michigan	Dr. J. H. Garnier [Ex.]	12238.
1 Kansas	Dr. J. H. Garnier [Ex.]	12116.

166. COLUBER FLAGELLIFORMIS, Holbr.

Garman, N. Amer. Snakes, p. 42.
Distribution—Southern parts of the United States.

2 Lesoya Texas, U. S. A.	Dr. J. H. Garnier. [Ex.]	12766-7.
1 N. America	Dr. J. H. Garnier [Ex.]	12237.

167. COLUBER TAENIATUS, Hallowell.

Garman, N. Amer. Snakes, p. 46.
Distribution—Western and Southern States and Mexico.

1 Texas	Dr. J. H. Garnier [Ex.]	12230.

168. COLUBER OBSOLETUS, Say.

Garman, N. Amer. Snakes, p. 54.
Distribution—Eastern United States to Texas.

1 Antonio Texas, U. S. A.	Dr. J. H Garnier	12244.
3 North America	No history	7349, 12761-2.

169. COLUBER GUTTATUS, Linn.

Garman N. Amer. Snakes, p. 55.
Distribution—Eastern United States.

3 Michigan, U. S. A.	Dr. J. H. Garnier	12231, 12239-40.

170. GONYOPHIS MARGARITATUS (Peters).

Boulenger, Ann. Mag. N. H. (6) viii, p. 290.
Distribution—Borneo and the Malay Peninsula.

1 Singapore	Raffles Museum (Davison)	13318.

171. XENELAPHIS HEXAGONATUS (Cantor).

Boulenger, p. 336.
Distribution—Burma, Malay Peninsula, Java, Sumatra and Borneo.

1 Penang	Purchased	7303.
1 Kwala Lumpor, Malay Peninsula	Raffles Mus. (Davison)	12312.
1 No loc.	No history	7302.

172. DENDROPHIS PICTUS, (Gmel.).

Boulenger, p. 337.
Distribution—India generally and Ceylon, Assam, Burma, Andamans, Nicobars, Siam, Malay Peninsula and Archipelago.

1 Chanda, C. P.	W. T. Blanford	7715.
1 Upper Godavery dist., C.P.	Dr. Goffrey	6909.
1 Aska, Ganjam dist. Madras	E. A. Minchin	12952.
1 Ceylon	W. Ferguson	7721.
1 Jashpur, Chota Nagpur	W. T. Blanford	7716.
1 Krishnagarh	R. de Dombal	7720.
1 Calcutta	E. Blyth, A. S. B.	7693.
6 Darjeeling	J. Gammie	7703-5, 7734-6.
1 Garo hills, Assam	Capt. Williamson	3945.
1 Garo hills, Assam	Col. H. H. Godwin Austen	7713.
1 Charapunji	J. H. Bourne	7700.
1 Narainpur, Assam	Duffla Exped. (Godwin Austen)	3998.
3 Sibsagar, Assam	S. E. Peal	4042, 4046, 7718.
4 Samaguting	Capt. Butler	7706-7, 7709-10.
1 Nazira, Assam	J. M. Foster	7701.
1 Naga hills	Lieut. J. Gregory	7717.
2 Assam	Major Jenkins, A. S. B.	7686-7.
1 Dilcosh N. Cachar	J. Inglis	11368.
1 Chittagong	B. Macdonald	7886.
1 Ramri Isle, Arakan	Capt. Abbott	7680.
1 Bhamo	Yunan Exped. (Anderson)	7696.
1 Upper Burma	F. Stoliczka	7698.
3 Tenasserim	Tenasserim Exped.	4074, 8614-5.
2 Mergui	Major Berdmore, A. S. B.	7684-5.
2 Andamans	Capt. Hodge, A. S. B.	7682-3.

2 Andamans	Col. Tytler, A. S. B.	7691-2.
1 Andamans	V. Ball	7714.
11 South Andamans	J. Wood Mason	4483-7, 4489-94.
3 Nicobars	F. A. de Roepstorff	7711-2, 12542.
5 Camorta, Nicobars	F. A. de Roepstorff	8886, 8897-8. 8890, 8894.
1 Perak	Museum Coll.	13242.
3 Malacca	Rev. E. Lindstedt, A. S. B.	7688-90.
4 Johore	Mus. Coll.	7896-9.
4 Singapore	Capt. T. S. Gardiner	12813, 13286. 13401-2.
1 Singapore	Mus. Coll.	7902.
1 Singapore	No history	4225.
3 Sinkip Isle, Sumatra	Mus. Coll.	7900-1, 7903.
1 Deli, Sumatra	Capt. T. S. Gardiner	12846.
6 Deli, Sumatra	L. Schwendler	11437, 11441. 11443-6.

173. DENDROPHIS SUBOCULARIS, Boul.

Boulenger, p. 338.
Distribution—Upper Burma.

1 Bhamo	Yunan Exped. (Anderson)	7697.

174. DENDROPHIS BIFRENALIS, Boul.

Boulenger, p. 338.
Distribution—Travancore and Ceylon.

1 Travancore	Trevandrum Museum	13504.

175. DENDROPHIS PUNCTULATA, Gray.

Krefft, Austr. Snakes, p. 23.
Distribution—Throughout Australia.

2 Queensland	Brisbane Mus.	11888, 11869.
1 N. S. Wales ?	Calcutta Exhibition	12626.

176. DENDRELAPHIS CAUDOLINEATUS, (Gray).

Boulenger, p. 339.
Distribution—The Wynaad in South India, Tenasserim, Malay Peninsula, Borneo, Sumatra and Celebes.

1 Mergui	Mergui Exped. (Anderson)	11582.
1 Penang	Purchased	7694.
1 Johore	Museum Coll.	7904.
2 Singapore	Capt. T. S. Gardiner	12637, 13164.
1 Deli, Sumatra	L. Schwendler	11442.

177. AHAETULLA SMARAGDINA, (Boie).

Günther, Cat. Col. Snakes, p. 151.
Distribution—West Africa.

1 Accra W. Africa	Berlin Mus. [Ex.]	7914.

178. AHAETULLA IRREGULARIS, (Leach).

Günther, Cat. Col. Snakes, p. 152.
Distribution—West Africa.

1 Africa	Netley Mus. [Ex.]	8726.

179. AHAETULLA LIOCERCUS, (Wied).

Günther, Cat. Col. Snakes, p. 153.
Distribution—The West Indies and Tropical South America.

1 West Indies	Netley Mus. [Ex.]	8729.

180. XENODON RHABDOCEPHALUS, (Wied).

Günther, Cat. Col. Snakes, p. 56.
Distribution—Tropical South America.

1 Bahia, Brazil	E. Gerard [P.]	12395.

181. PSEUDOXENODON MACROPS, (Bly.).

Boulenger, p. 340.
Distribution—Sikkim, Assam, Burma.

2 Darjeeling	Major W. S. Sherwill, A. S. B.	7506-7.
(TYPES OF THE SPECIES, Blyth).		
2 Darjeeling 5000 ft.	J. Gammie	7556-7.
(TYPES OF TROPIDONOTUS SIKKIMENSIS, Anders.).		
12 Darjeeling	J. Gammie	7543-5, 7555. 7746-7, 7781-3. 8792-3, 8816.
3 Darjeeling	J. Anderson	7535-7.
1 Darjeeling 7000 ft.	J. S. Gamble	12023.
2 Duffla hills	Duffla Exped. (Godwin Austen)	3999-4000.
3 Charapunji	J. H. Bourne	7538-40.
1 Ramri Isle, Arakan	Capt. Abbott, A. S. B.	7502.
(TYPE OF TROPIDONOTUS ANGUSTICEPS, Blyth).		
1 Tenasserim	Tenasserim Exped.	5522.

182. TROPIDONOTUS MODESTUS, Gunth.

Boulenger, p. 343.
Distribution—Assam and Yunan.

5 Charapunji, Assam	J. H. Bourne	4273-6, 4278.
1 Muangla, Yunan	Yunan Exped. (Anderson)	4272.
1 Hotha, Yunan	Yunan Exped. (Anderson)	4271.
1 Yunan	Yunan Exped. (Anderson)	4193.

183. TROPIDONOTUS PLATYCEPS, Bly.

Boulenger, p. 343.
Distribution—Himalayas from Kashmir to Assam.

2 Kashmir	Yarkand Exped. (Stoliczka)	8574-5.

1 Murree	Yarkand Exped. (Stoliczka)	8620.
3 Kulu N. W. Himalayas	F. Stoliczka [P.]	7485-7.
2 Darjeeling	Capt. W. S. Sherwill	7482-3.

(TYPE OF THE SPECIES, Blyth.).

16 Darjeeling	J. Gammie	7488-9, 7492-501, 7745, 8484-5, 8803.
1 Kurseong, Darjeeling dist.	O. L. Fraser	13508.
1 "Allahabad"	J. Cockburn	8622.
1 No loc.	No history	12055.

184. TROPIDONOTUS BEDDOMII, Gunth.

Boulenger, p. 344.
Distribution—The Hills of Southern India.

1 Koppa, Mysore	W. M. Daly	13532.
1 Wynaad, Malabar dist.	E. Gerard [P.]	12383.
1 Travancore	Col. R. H. Beddome	4315.
1 Tinnevelli hills	Col. R. H. Beddome	4418.
3 Madras Pres.	Col. R. H. Beddome	7559-61.
2 No loc.	F. Stoliczka	3962, 4051.

185. TROPIDONOTUS PARALLELUS, Boul.

Boulenger, p. 345.
Distribution—Sikkim, Assam and Yunnan.

1 Darjeeling	J. Anderson	7490.
1 Charapunji, Assam.	J. H. Bourne	8724.
1 Shillong, Assam	Major C. R. Cock	3852.
2 Muangla valley, Yunan	Yunan Exped. 1868 (Andersou)	8531, 8538.
7 Hotha, Yunan	Yunan Exped. 1868 (Anderson)	8532-7, 8540.
1 Ponsee, Yunan	Yunan Exped. 1868 (Anderson)	8539.
1 "Madras hills"?	Col. R. H. Beddome.	4397.

186. TROPIDONOTUS CHRYSARGUS, Schleg.

Boulenger, p. 345; Sclater, J. A. S. B. lx, p. 239.
Distribution—Sikkim, Assam, Burma, South China, Malay Peninsula, Java, Borneo and Sumatra.

1 Mooleyit Mt. 5-6000 ft. Tenasserim	Tenasserim Exped. (Limborg).	8972.
1 Tenasserim	Tenasserim Exped. (Limborg)	6847.
1 Meta, Tavoy dist.	Mus. Coll.	12841.
1 Semudaing, Tavoy dist.	Mus. Coll.	12823.
3 Egaya, Tavoy dist.	Mus. Coll.	12648-50.
1 Tavoy dist.	Mus. Coll	12729.
1 Minthanthonng, Mergui	Mergui Exped. (Anderson)	11547.
1 King's Isle, Mergui	Mergui Exped. (Anderson)	11545.
4 Sullivan Isle, Mergui	Mergui Exped. (Anderson)	11542-4, 11549.

187. TROPIDONOTUS NIGROCINCTUS, Bly.

Boulenger, p. 346; Sclater, J. A. S. B. lx, p. 239.
Distribution—Pegu and Tenasserim.

3 Pegu	Major Berdmore, A. S. B.	7479-81.

(TYPES OF THE SPECIES, Blyth.).

2 Tenasserim	Tenasserim Exped.	4477, 55.02
1 Meta, Tavoy	Mus. Coll.	12839.
2 Tavoy	Mus. Coll.	12678, 12728.
1 Kings Isle, Mergui	Mergui Exped. (Anderson)	11857.

188. TROPIDONOTUS SUBMINIATUS, Schleg.

Boulenger, p. 347.

Distribution—Sikkim, Assam, Burma, Yunan, South China, Malay Peninsula and Java.

1 Darjeeling	Capt. Jerdan	7426.
1 Nagaisurie, Jalpi. dist.	G. W. Shillingford	12667.
1 Garo hills	Capt. Williamson	3936.
1 Charapnnji	Col. H. H. Godwin Austen	7427.
1 Goalpara, Assam	H. L. Hanghton	3196.
1 Naga hills	Lieut. Gregory	7420.
5 Samaguting	Capt. J. Bntler	7421-5.
1 Nazira, Sibsagar dist.	J. M. Foster	7409.
2 Assam	J. Robinson	7404-5.
1 Munipur	R. D. Oldham	11937.
1 Chittagong	B. Macdonald	7887.
3 Muangla, Yunan	Ynnan Exped. (Anderson)	7429-31.
1 Hotha, Ynnan	Ynnan Exped. (Anderson)	4190.
1 Nantin Valley, Yunan	Ynnan Exped. (Anderson)	4195.
1 Yunan	Yunan Exped. (Anderson)	4189.
1 Pegu	W. Theobald	7419.
1 Burma	W. Theobald	7408.
4 Monlmein	Capt. Hood	7414, 7416, 7432-3.
1 Mooleyit Mt. 3500 ft. Tenasserim	Tenasserim Exped. (Limborg)	4096.
3 Tenasserim	Tenasserim Exped. (Limborg)	4076-8.
2 Semudaing, Tavoy	Mus. Coll.	12822-5.
1 Egaya, Tavoy	Mus. Coll.	12651.
2 Tavoy	Mns. Coll.	12677, 12710.
1 Poinednng, Mergui	Mergui Exped. (Anderson)	11583.
1 Mergui	Mergui Exped. (Anderson)	11546.
1 "Madras hills"?	Col. R. H. Beddome	4398.

189. TROPIDONOTUS HIMALAYANUS, Gunth.

Boulenger, p. 347; Sclater, J. A. S. B. lx, p. 240.

Distribution—Nepal, Sikkim, Assam and Burma.

8 Darjeeling 3200 ft.	J. Gammie	7542, 7547-53.
1 Darjeeling 4000 ft.	Capt. Jerdan	7554.
1 Darjeeling	T. Johnston	8435.
1 Darjeeling	No hist.	4226.
2 Garo hills, Assam	N. Belletty	7509-10.
2 Charapunji	Col. H. H. Godwin Austen	7410, 7546.
2 Charapunji	J. H. Bourne	7511-12.
2 Khasia hills	Col. H. H. Godwin Austen	7411-12.
1 Nazira, Sibsagar dist.	J. M. Foster	7541.
4 Sibsagar dist.	S. E. Peal	3193, 4035, 7407, 7428
1 Assam	W. Robinson, A. S. B.	7403.
2 Moulmein	Capt. Hood	7417-8.
1 "Anamalais"	Col. R. H. Beddome	4029.

190. TROPIDONOTUS MONTICOLA, Jerdon.

Boulenger, p. 348.

Distribution—Southern India.

1 Madras Pr.	Col. R. H. Beddome	7558.
1 No loc.	F. Stoliczka	3957.

191. TROPIDONOTUS STOLATUS, (Linn.).

Boulenger, p. 348.

Distribution—Throughout India from the Himalayas to Ceylon, Assam, Burma, Nicobars, Malay Peninsula and South China.

1 Dehra Doon	J. Wood Mason	13239.
4 Katmandu, Nepal	Mus. Coll.	7444-7.
1 Karachi	Karachi Mus. [Ex.]	8649.
1 Sipri, Gwalior	F. J. Daley	13241.
1 Nowgong, C. P.	F. J. Daley	13411.
1 Ellore, Godavery dist.	W. T. Blanford	8852.
6 Ganjam dist., Madr.	V. Ball	8857-9, 8853-5.
1 Bangalore	E. A. Minchin	12945.
2 Conoor, Nilgiris	F. Day	4303-4.
1 Madamally, Malabar	Col. R. H. Beddome	4437.
1 Tinnevelli dist.	Col. R. H. Beddome	4404.
1 Travancore	Trevandrum Museum	13506.
1 Madras Pr.	F. Stoliczka	7474.
1 Columbo, Ceylon	W. Ferguson	7470.
1 Galle, Ceylon	S. Ransom	11394.
1 Ceylon	E. F. Kelaart, A. S. B.	7438.
3 Singbhum	V. Ball	8782-4.
2 Govindpur, Manbhum dist.	E. V. Westmacott	7448-9.
1 Doomakonda, (Barrakur)	F. J. Buchanan	7450.
3 Darbhangah	C. Maries	11932-4.
1 Calcutta	Sir J. Fayrer	7477.
1 Calcutta	J. Moseley, A. S. B.	7440.
3 Calcutta	No hist., A. S. B.	7434-6.
1 Nr. Calcutta	A. C. L. Carlleyle, A. S. B.	7437.
1 Botanical Gardens, Calcutta	J. Anderson	8846.
1 Botanical Gardens, Calcutta	No history	7475.
1 Port Canning	W. L. Swinhoe	7476.
1 Port Canning	J. Wood Mason	8851.
1 Dacca	N. Belletty	8785.
3 Kaligunj, Rungpur dist.	W. Dodgson	7456-8.
1 Kuch Behar	Messrs. Gillanders Arbuthnot and Co.	12776.
1 Shillong, Assam	Duffla Exped. (Godwin Austen)	3997.
1 Tezpur, Assam	Duffla Exped. (Godwin Austen)	3996.
2 Nazira, Sibsagar dist.	J. M. Foster	7455, 7473.
6 Sibsagar dist., Assam	E. Peal	4030-3, 7472, 8789.
1 Dibrugarh	J. Meredith	7471.
4 Assam	Col. H. H. Godwin Austen	7451-4.
3 Cachar	Mus. Coll. (Sheik Harrie)	7462, 7464-5.

1 Bhamo	Yunan Exped.	4188.
3 Mandalay	Sir P. Sladen	7459-61.
1 Meiktalla, Upper Burma	Gen. H. Collett	13240.
4 Prome	W. Dumeroy	7466-9.
3 Burma	N. S. Bligh	7441-3.
1 Hatsiega, Tenasserim	Tenasserim Exped. (Limborg)	8542.
2 Camorta, Nicobars	F. A. de Roepstorff	8891, 8893.
2 No hist.	No loc.	7533-4.

(TYPES OF TROPIDONOTUS OLIVACEUS, Blyth).

1 No hist.	No loc.	12058.

192. TROPIDONOTUS PISCATOR, (Schneid.).

Boulenger, p. 349.

Distribution—Throughout the Indian Empire from Quetta to Tenasserim, South China, the Malay Peninsula and Archipelego.

2 Quetta	Sir O. B. C. St. John	11692-3.
1 Lahore	No history	13167.
1 Jeypore, Rjpt.	R. Pattoon	7681.
1 Ajmere	Sir O. B. C. St. John	13478.
1 Mt. Aboo, Rjpt.	Dr. G. S. Sutherland	8631.
1 Kathgodam below Naini Tal	W. L. Sclater	13205.
1 Agra dist.	Agra Museum	7388.
3 Allahabad	J. Cockburn	7392-4.
2 Goruckpore dist , N. W. P.	A. C. L. Carlleyle	4679-80.
1 Korba, Bilaspur, C. P.	W. T. Blanford	7396.
1 Canara dist.	F. Day	4287.
2 Travancore	Purchased	7389-90.
2 Galle, Ceylon	J. Anderson	7365-6.
1 20 M. from Galle	J. Anderson	7369.
1 Galle	S. Ransom	11393.
1 Ceylon	H. Nevill	8670.
1 Govindpur, Manbhum dist.	E. V. Westmacott	7391.
1 Barrakur	F. Buchanan	7386.
1 Darbhangah	C. Maries	11931.
1 Calcutta	J. Anderson	11953.
1 Port Canning	W. Swinhoe	7385.
2 Sundarbans	A. C. L. Carlleyle	7361-2.
4 Dacca	Mus. Coll.	7380-3.
3 Kaliganj, Rungpur dist.	W. Dodgson	7377-9.
2 Charapunji, Assam	J. H. Bourne	7397-8.
2 Samaguting	Capt. J. Butler	7367-8.
1 Nazira, Sibsagar dist.	J. M. Foster	7360.
3 Sibsagar, Assam	S. E. Peal	4024-6.
1 Dilcosh, N. Cachar	J. Inglis	11366.
3 Hailacandi, S. Cachar	C. H. Dreyer	4687-9.
1 Bhamo	Yunan Exped. (Anderson)	7363.
1 Tsitkaw, U. Burma	Yunan Exped. (Anderson)	8675.
1 Mandalay	Yunan Exped. (Anderson)	7364.
1 Mandalay	Sir P. Sladen	7387.
2 Upper Pegu	W. T. Blanford, A. S. B.	7357-8.
1 Pegu	W. Theobald	7375.
1 Moulmein	Capt. Hood	4111.
1 Tenasserim	Tenasserim Exped. (Limborg)	5521.

1 Andamans	Capt. Homfray, A. S. B.	7373.
2 Andamans	Major Ford	7372, 7384.
1 Andamans	Col. R. C. Tytler	7402.

(TYPE OF T. TYTLERI BLYTH, AND OF T. STRIOLATUS, Theob.).

1 Andamans	Col. R. C. Tytler	7359.
2 Andamans	F. Stoliczka	7370-1.
1 Andamans	V. Ball	7395.
1 Andamans	G. E. Dobson	8916.
4 S. Andamans	J. Wood Mason	4495-8.

193. TROPIDONOTUS PUNCTULATUS, Gunth.

Boulenger, p. 350.
Distribution—Burma.

1 Rangoon (Fowle)	W. Theobald, A. S. B.	7579.

(TYPE OF FOWLEA PEGUENSIS, Theobald).

1 Mergui	Mergui Exped. (Anderson)	11570.

194. TROPIDONOTUS PLUMBICOLOR, Cantor.

Boulenger, p. 351; Sclater, J. A. S. B. lx, p. 240.
Distribution—Southern India and Ceylon extending northwards to Mt. Aboo and the Central Provinces.

2 Mt. Aboo, Rjpt.	Dr. G. S. Sutherland	7514-5.
2 Nowgong, C. P.	F. J. Daley	13279, 13410.
1 Upper Godavery dist. C. P.	Dr. Goffney	7517.
1 Koppa, Mysore	W. M. Daly	13533.
1 Shevaroy hills, Salem dist.	B. Daly	13526.
1 Conoor, Nilgiri hills	F. Day	4302.
1 Anamalai hills	Col. R. H. Beddome	4394.
1 Tinnevelli hills	Col. R. H. Beddome	4428.
1 Madras Pr.	W. Davison	8737.
1 W. of Galle, Ceylon	J. Anderson	7516.
1 No loc.	E. Gerard [P.]	12362.
1 No loc.	No hist.	8765.

195. TROPIDONOTUS VIBAKARI, Boie.

Günther, Cat. Col. Snakes, p. 80.
Distribution—North-East Asia, extending to Tenasserim.

1 Tavoy	Museum Collector	12680

196. TROPIDONOTUS PEALII, Scl.

Sclater, J. A. S. B. lx, p. 241.
Distribution—Assam.

2 Sibsagar, Assam	S. E. Peal	4034, 4043.

(TYPES OF THE SPECIES, SCLATER).

197. TROPIDONOTUS NICOBARENSIS, Scl.

Sclater, J. A. S. B. lx, p. 241.
Distribution—Nicobar Islands.

1 Camorta, Nicobars	F. A. de Roepstorff	8895.

(TYPE OF THE SPECIES, SCLATER).

198. TROPIDONOTUS RHODOMELAS, Boie.

Blanford, P. Z. S. 1881, p. 221.
Distribution—Malay Peninsula, Sumatra, Java and Celebes.

5 Singapore	Capt. T. S. Gardiner	12642, 12807, 12809, 12812, 13285.
1 Singapore	W. Davison	13329.
1 Sinkip Isle, Sumatra	J. Wood Mason	4238.
1 No loc.	No. hist., A. S. B.	7568.

(TYPE OF T. MORTONI, Theobald).

199. TROPIDONOTUS TRIANGULIGERUS, Schleg.

Günther, Rept. Brit. Ind., p. 261 ; Sclater, J. A. S. B. lx, p. 242.
Distribution—Tenasserim, Malay Peninsula, Sumatra, Java and Borneo.

2 Kings Isle, Mergui.	Mergui Exped. (Anderson)	11560-1.
1 Tenasserim	Tenasserim Exped. (Limborg)	4079.
1 Palian, Malay Peninsula	Raffles Mus. (Davison)	13328.
1 Sinkip Isle, Sumatra	J. Wood Mason	4236.

200. TROPIDONOTUS LEUCOMELAS, Gunth.

Günther, Reptiles Brit. Ind., p. 271.
Distribution—Malay Peninsula.

1 Penang	Hongkong Mus. [Ex.]	12696.

201. TROPIDONOTUS CONSPICILLATUS, Gunth.

Günther, P. Z. S. 1872, p. 596.
Distribution—Borneo and Sumatra.

1 Sinkip Isle, Sumatra	J. Wood Mason	4237.

202. TROPIDONOTUS HYDRUS, (Pallas).

Blanford, Persia, p. 419.
Distribution—South Russia, Western Asia through Persia to Eastern Turkestan.

1 Damascus	J. Anderson	11141.
2 Enzeli, Caspian Sea	W. T. Blanford	8466, 8717.
1 Anan Mazendaran, N. Persia	Persian Coll. (Blanford)	8464.
1 Tang-i-Kerim, E. of Shiraz	Persiau Coll. (Blanford)	8465.

1 Mastagh Range, Gilgit, 8,000 ft.	G. M. Giles	12873.
12 Yangihissar, East Turkestan	Yarkand Exped. (Stoliczka)	8503-6, 8508-10, 8512-16.
1 Kashgar	Yarkand Exped. (Stoliczka)	8703.
2 Eastern Turkestan	J. Scully	13195-6.
2 No loc.	No hist., A. S. B.	7503-4.

(TYPES OF T. ANGUSTICEPS, BLY.).

203. TROPIDONOTUS NATRIX, (Linn.).

Blanford, Persia, p. 418.

Distribution—Throughout Europe, N. Africa and Western Asia as far as Northern Persia.

5 Resht., N. Persia	Sir O. B. C. St. John	7528-32.
1 Enzeli, N. Persia	W. T. Blanford	3498.
1 Epping forest, England	O. L. Fraser	12018.
1 England	R. Hancock, A. S. B.	7526.
1 England	E. Blyth, A. S. B.	7527.
1 Europe	G. E. Dobson [Ex.]	8770.

204. TROPIDONOTUS TIGRINUS, Boie.

Günther, Cat. Col. Snakes, p. 71.

Distribution—China and Japan.

1 Japan	R. Hungerford	11452.

205. TROPIDONOTUS VITTATUS, (Linn.).

Günther, Cat. Col. Snakes, p. 67.

Distribution—China and Java.

2 Java	F. Stoliczka	8357-8.

206. TROPIDONOTUS SAURITA, (Linn.).

Garman, N. Amer. Snakes, p. 23.

Distribution—Eastern half of North America from Canada to Mexico.

1 Lucknow, Ont. Canada	Dr. J. H. Garnier [Ex.]	12763.
2 Lake Erie, Canada	Dr. J. H. Garnier [Ex.]	12266-7.
1 Worcester, Mass., U. S. A.	Dr. J. H. Garnier [Ex.]	12768.
1 Chehnahua, Mexico	Dr. J. H. Garnier [Ex.]	12265.
1 North America	Dr. J. H. Garnier [Ex.]	12120.
1 " "	E. Gerard, [P.]	12385.

207. TROPIDONOTUS SIRTALIS, (Linn.).

Garman, N. Amer. Snakes, p. 23.

Distribution—Throughout North America extending southwards to Panama.

1 Prince Edwards Isle	Netley Mus. [Ex.]	8727.
4 Huron Co., Ont. Canada	Dr. J. H. Garnier [Ex.]	12275-6, 12281-2.
5 Lake St. Clair, Ont. Canada	Dr. J. H. Garnier [Ex.]	12119, 12271-2, 12279-80.

16 Ontario, Canada	Dr. J. H. Garnier [Ex.]	12236, 12247-61.
3 N. Carolina, U. S. A.	Rev. F. Fitzgerald, A. S. B.	7523-5.
2 Lesoya, Texas, U. S. A.	Dr. J. H. Garnier [Ex.]	12759-60.
3 Helotes, Texas, U. S. A.	Dr. J. H. Garnier [Ex.]	12241-3.
2 Iowa, U. S. A.	Dr. J. H. Garnier [Ex.]	12207-8.
6 Oregon, U. S. A.	Dr. J. H. Garnier [Ex.]	12113-5, 12117-8, 12283.
1 N. America	Dr. J. H. Garnier [Ex.]	12264.

208. TROPIDONOTUS SIPEDON, (Linn.).

Garman, N. Amer. Snakes, p. 25.
Distribution—N. America from Canada to Mexico.

3 Lake Huron, Ont. Canada	Dr. J. H. Garnier [Ex.]	12233-5.
3 Lake St. Clair, Ont. Canada	Dr. J. H. Garnier [Ex.]	12111, 12277-8.
1 Ontario	Dr. J. H. Garnier [Ex.]	12311.
5 N. Carolina	Rev. F. Fitzgerald	7518-22.
1 Texas	Dr. J. H. Garnier [Ex.]	12262.

209. TROPIDONOTUS LEBERIS, (Linn.).

Garman, N. Amer. Snakes, p. 27.
Distribution—N. America.

2 Lake St. Clair, Ont. Canada	Dr. J. H. Garnier	12198-9.

210. STORERIA OCCIPITOMACULATA, (Storer).

Garman, N. Amer. Snakes, p. 30.
Distribution—Eastern States and Canada.

2 Ontario, Canada	Dr. J. H. Garnier [Ex.]	12223-4.

211. STORERIA DEKAYI, (Holbrook).

Garman, N. Amer. Snakes, p. 31.
Distribution—N. America from Canada to Mexico.

3 Huron Co., Ont. Canada	Dr. J. H. Garnier [Ex.]	12225-7.
1 No loc.	No hist., A. S. B.	7508.

212. HELICOPS SCHISTOSUS, (Daud.).

Boulenger, p. 352.
Distribution—South India, Ceylon, Bengal, Burma, Yunan and the Malay Peninsula.

1 Ceylon	W. Ferguson	7580.
3 Galle, Ceylon and Port Canning, Bengal.	J. Anderson and W. Swinhoe	7581-3.
3 Lower Bengal	No hist., A. S. B.	7569-71.
1 Lower Bengal	A. C. L. Carlleyle	7578.
3 Hotha and Muangla valleys, Yunan	Yunan Exped (Anderson)	4191-2, 4196.
1 No loc.	No hist.	8683.

213. URANOPS ANGULATUS, (Fitz.).

Gray, Cat. Snakes, B. M., p. 68.
Distribution—Tropical South America.

Demarara	D. Carruthers	3194.
Bahia, Brazil	E. Gerard [P.]	12380.

214. HYDROPS ABACURUS, (Holbrook).

Garman, N. Amer. Snakes, p. 36.
Distribution—South Western States of N. America.

1 N. Carolina	Rev. F. Fitzgerald, A. S. B.	8196.

215. HYDROPS EYTHROGRAMMUS, (Daud.).

Garman, N. Amer. Snakes, p. 35.
Distribution—South Eastern States of N. America.

1 N. America	No bistory, A. S. B.	8177.

216. XENOCHROPHIS CERASOGASTER, (Cantor).

Boulenger, p. 353.
Distribution—Bengal, Assam, Burma and Malay Peninsula.

3 Lower Bengal	No hist., A. S. B.	7584-6.
2 Goalpara, Assam	H. L. Hanghton	7587-8.

Subfamily DASYPELTINAE.

217. DASYPELTIS SCABRA, (Linn.).

Günther, Cat. Col. Snakes, p. 142.
Distribution—South Africa.

1 Cape Colony	Berlin Mus. [Ex.]	7916.
1 Africa	Netley Mus. [Ex.]	8546.

Subfamily ACROCHORDINAE.

218. CHERSYDRUS GRANULATUS, (Schneid.).

Boulenger, p. 355.
Distribution—River-mouths and Coasts of India, Burma, the Malay Peninsula and Archipelego to New Guinea.

1 Hijili, Midnapur dist.	H. L. Haughton, A. S. B.	8091.
1 Singapore	Derrick Spon	12968.
1 India	E. Gerard [P.]	12364.

Subfamily DIPSADINAE.

219. DIPSAS TRIGONATA, (Schneid.).

Boulenger, p. 358.
Distribution—The Himalayas, and throughout India extending to Beluchistan.

1 Subathu, nr. Simla	Rev. Cave Brown, A. S. B.	7836.
2 Karachi	Karachi Mus. [Ex.]	3186, 8458.

2 Jaipur, Rajpt.	R. Pattoon	8553-4.
1 Ajmere, Rajpt.	Sir O. B. C. St. John	13479.
1 Nowgong, C. P.	F. J. Daley	13409.
1 Aska, Ganjam dist.	E. A. Minchin	12942.
1 Bangalore	E. A. Minchin	12943.
1 Anamalai hills	Col. R. H. Beddome	4431.
1 S. India	E. Gerard [P.]	12379.
1 Balasor	J. Cleghorn	13398.
1 Manbhum	V. Ball	7840.
1 Kolassy, Purneah dist.	G. W. Shillingford	8710.
2 Calcutta	Sir F. Haines	11384.
1 Botanical Gardens	Purchased	8961.
3 Bengal	No history	7843-5.
2 No loc.	No hist., A. S. B.	7846-7.
1 No loc.	No hist.	8646.

220. DIPSAS CEYLONENSIS, (Gunth.).

Boulenger, p. 359.

Distribution—Southern India and Ceylon.

3 Koppa, Mysore	W. M. Daly	13534-6.
1 Anamalai hills	Col. R. H. Beddome	4430.
2 Madras Pres.	Col. R. H. Beddome	8047, 8387.
1 No loc.	E. Gerard [P.]	12392.

221. DIPSAS MULTIFASCIATUS, Bly.

Sclater, J. A. S. B. lx, p. 243.

Distribution—The Himalayas from Simla to Sikkim.

1 Subathu, nr. Simla	Rev. Cave Brown, A. S. B. (TYPE OF THE SPECIES, Blyth.).	7861.
2 Mussooree	W. E. Hillier	8579-80.
1 Naini Tal	V. Ball	11431.
2 Darjeeling	J. Gammie.	7859-60.

222. DIPSAS GOKOOL, Gray.

Boulenger, p. 360.

Distribution—Bengal, Assam and Penang.

1 Jessore	R. W. G. Frith, A. S. B.	7837.
2 Bengal	No hist.	7841-2.
3 Samaguting, Assam	Capt. J. Butler	7923-5.
2 Sibsagar	S. E. Peal	7921-2.
1 No loc.	No hist., A. S. B.	7838.
3 No loc.	No hist.	8428-30.

223. DIPSAS MULTIMACULATA, Schleg.

Boulenger, p. 360.

Distribution—Burma, Southern China, Siam, Malay Peninsula, and Islands.

1 Rangoon	Col. Hawkes	6701.
2 Pegu	W. Theobald	7857-8.

1 Pegu ?	F. Stoliczka	8363.
1 Moulmein	Capt. I. H. Hood	8564.
1 Hongkong	W. G. Bowring, A. S. B.	7854.
2 No loc.	No hist., A. S. B.	7855-6.

224. DIPSAS HEXAGONATUS, Bly.

Boulenger, p. 361.
Distribution—Sikkim and Terai, Assam and Upper Burma.

25 Darjeeling dist. 3500 ft.	J. Gammie	7737-8, 7862-73, 7875-9. 8473-7, 8817.
3 Darjeeling dist.	Capt. Jerdan	7880, 7934, 8446.
1 Nagaisuri, Jalpi. dist.	G. W. Shillingford	12879.
1 Buxa, Jalpi. dist.	Mus. Coll.	12565.
1 Goalpara, Assam	H. L. Haughton	7932.
1 Sibsagar	S. E. Peal	7933.
1 Dilcosh, N. Cachar	J. Inglis	11367.
1 Meiktalla, U. Burma	Gen. H. Collett	13250.

225. DIPSAS CYANEA, (Dum. & Bibr.).

Boulenger, p. 361 ; Sclater, J. A. S. B. lx, p. 244.
Distribution—Sikkim, Assam and Burma.

1 Assam	W. Robinson, A. S. B. (TYPE OF D. NIGROMARGINATA, Bly.).	7853.
1 Cachar	Mus. Coll.	7926.
1 Tavoy	Mus. Coll.	12705.

226. DIPSAS CYNODON, Cuv.

Sclater, J. A. S. B. lx, p. 244.
Distribution—Assam, Burma, Malay Peninsula and Islands.

1 Garo hills	Capt. Williamson	8662.
1 Samaguting, Assam	Capt. J. Butler	7831.
1 Cachar	Mus. Coll.	8718.
1 Thayetmyo, Burma	W. T. Blanford, A. S. B.	7832.
2 Burma-Siam hills	Mus. Coll.	12777-8.
1 Mergui	W. Theobald	7830.
1 Malacca	E. Lindstedt, A. S. B.	7829.

227. DIPSAS FUSCA, (Gray).

Krefft., Austr. Snakes, p. 26.
Distribution—Assam, the Andamans, Java, Celebes, N. Guinea and N. Australia.

1 Charapunji, Assam	Col. H. H. Godwin Austen	8048.
3 Port Blair, Andamans	Capt. W. Hodge, A. S. B.	7928-30.
1 Andamans	J. Wood-Mason	8641.

228. DIPSAS FORSTENII, (Dum. & Bibr.).

Boulenger, p. 362.
Distribution—Throughout India and Ceylon.

1 20 Miles W. of Galle, Ceylon	J. Anderson	7849

1 Govindpur, Manbhum	E. V. Westmacott	7850.
2 Manbhum	F. S. Buchanan	7851-2.
1 Purneah	G. W. Shillingford	13542.
2 No loc.	No hist.	7215, 7848.

229. DIPSAS RHINOPOMA, Blanf.

Blanford, Persia, p. 424.
Distribution—South Persia.

1 Karman, S. E. Persia	Persian Coll. (Blanford).	3500.

(TYPE OF THE SPECIES, Blanford).

230. DIPSAS BOOPS, Gunth.

Günther, Reptiles Brit. Ind. p. 309.
Distribution—Malay Peninsula and Islands.

1 Sunji Ujong, Malay P.	Raffles Museum (Davison)	13320.

231. DIPSAS CENCHOA, (Linn.).

Günther, Cat. Col. Snakes, p. 174.
Distribution—South America.

1 S. America ?	Brit. Mus. [Ex.]	4741.

232. LEPTODEIRA RUFESCENS, (Gm.).

Günther, Cat. Col. Snakes, p. 165.
Distribution—Africa.

1 Zanzibar Coast.	Berlin Mus. [Ex.]	7919.
1 No loc.	No hist.	8666.

233. THAMNODYNASTES NATTERI, (Wied).

Günther, Cat. Col. Snakes, p. 164.
Distribution—Tropical South America.

1 Demarara	D. Carruthers	8767.

234. ELACHISTODON WESTERMANNI, Reinh.

Boulenger, p. 363.
Distribution—Bengal.

1 Purneah	G. W. Shillingford	7212.

235. TANTILLA GRACILIS, Baird and Girard.

Garman, N. Amer. Snakes, p. 87.
Distribution—Southern United States.

2 Texas	Dr. J. H. Garnier [Ex.]	12284-5.

236. SCYTALE CORONATUM, Dum. & Bibr.

Günther, Cat. Col. Snakes, p. 187.
Distribution—Tropical South America.

1 South America	Netley Mus. [Ex.]	8758.
1 South America	E. Gerard [P.]	12394.

237. PSAMMODYNASTES PULVERULENTUS (Boie).

Boulenger, p. 363.
Distribution—Sikkim, Assam, Burma, Cochin China, Malay Peninsula and Islands.

6 Darjeeling dist. 17-1900 ft.	J. Gammie	7648-52, 7731.
27 Charapunji, Assam	J. H. Bourne	7615-25, 7632-47.
6 Charapunji	Col. H. H. Godwin Austen	7653-4, 7662-5.
3 Khasia hills	Col. H. H. Godwin Austen	7626-8.
1 Samaguting	Capt. J. Butler	7659.
2 Sibsagar	S. E Peal	6908, 7629.
1 Assam	W. Robinson, A. S. B.	7605.
3 Pegu	W. Theobald	7656-8.
3 Pegu	F. Stoliczka	8364-6.
1 Moulmein	Capt. J. H. Hood	4110.
1 Tavoy	Mus. Coll.	12679.
2 King Isle, Mergui	Mergui Exped. (Anderson)	11540-1.
3 Burma	No hist. A. S. B.	7607 7611-12.
1 Burma	W. Theobald	7630.
1 Dehli, Sumatra	L. Schwendler	11433.
1 No loc.	No hist.	7604.

238. PSAMMODYNASTES PICTUS, Gunth.

Günther, Cat. Col. Snakes, p. 251.
Distribution—Malay Peninsula, Java and Borneo.

3 Johore, Malay P.	J. Meldrum	4660, 4662-3.
1 Java	F. Stoliczka	8682.

239. COELOPELTIS LACERTINA, (Wagl.).

Schreiber Herp. Europ., p. 221.
Distribution—Circum-Mediterranean Countries.

1 Samaria, Palestine	J. Anderson	11243.
1 Africa	Netley Mus.	8668.

240. TAPHROMETOPUM LINEOLATUM, Brandt.

Blanford, Persia, p. 422.
Distribution—Persia, Afghanistan and Eastern and Western Turkestan.

1 nr Saadatabad, S. E. Persia	Persian Coll. (Blanford)	3499.
1 Kandahar ?	Rev. Warneford	11395.
1 Zindijan nr. Tirphul	Afghan. B. Comm. (Aichison)	13135.

2 nr Tirphul	Afghan. Bound. Comm. (Aichison)	13136.
1 Beshterek E. Turkestan	Yarkand Exped. (Stoliczka)	8595.

241. PSAMMOPHIS LEITHII, Gunth.

Boulenger, p. 365.

Distribution—Arabia, Persia, Beluchistan, Afghanistan, Sind, Punjab, Cutch and Rajpootana.

2 Bushire, Persia	W. D. Cumming	13421-2.
1 Niriz E. of Shiraz	Persian Coll. (Blanford)	8585.
1 Karman, Persia	Persian Coll. (Blanford)	4614.
1 nr. Bam, S. E. Persia	Persian Coll. (Blanford)	4612.
1 Isfandak, Baluchistan	Persian Coll. (Blanford)	4613.
1 Pishin, Baluchistan	Persian Coll. (Blanford)	8584.
1 Quetta	Sir O. B. C. St. John	11697.
1 Chāman, S. Afghan.	J. A. Murray	11421.
1 Rajanpur, Panjab	D. D. Cunningham	8593.
2 Sukkur, Sind	F. Stoliczka	7602-3.

(TYPE OF P. SINDIANUS, Stol.).

3 Karachi	Karachi Mus. [Ex.]	8440, 8663, 8705.
1 Lower Sind	F. Fedden	10974.
1 Ken R., Banda, N. W. P.	J. Cockburn	11453.
1 Cutch	F. Stoliczka	7596.

242. PSAMMOPHIS CONDANARUS, (Merr.).

Boulenger, p. 366.

Distribution—Himalayas, Northern India and Burma.

1 Simla	F. Stoliczka	7601.
1 Cutch	F. Stoliczka [Ex.]	7597.
2 Lower Bengal	Mr. Russell, A. S. B.	7594-5.
1 Proome, Burma	A. Dunn	7598.
1 Bassein, Pegu	W. Theobald, A. S. B.	7600.

(TYPE OF PHAYREA ISABELLINA, Theobald).

1 No loc.	No hist.	8730.

243. PSAMMOPHIS SIBILANS (Linn.).

Schreiber, Herp. Europ., p. 217.

Distribution—South Russia, Western Asia and throughout Africa.

1 Joppa, Palestine	Berlin Mus. [Ex.]	7915.
1 Somaliland	Capt. Speke, A. S. B.	7593.
1 West Africa	Netley Mus. [Ex.]	8462.
1 Cape of Good Hope	Surgeon, H. M. S. Galetea	8567.

244. PSAMMOPHIS CRUCIFER, (Merr.).

Günther, Cat. Col. Snakes, p. 135.

Distribution—South Africa.

1 Africa	Netley Mus. [Ex.]	8709.

245. PSAMMOPHIS ELEGANS, (Shaw.).

Günther, Cat. Col. Snakes, p. 138.
Distribution—West Africa.

1 West Africa	Berlin Mus. [Ex.]	7918.
1 No loc.	No hist.	8678.

246. DRYOPHIS PERROTETI, (Dum. & Bibr.).

Boulenger, p. 368.
Distribution—Southern India and Burma?

3 Nilgiris	W. Theobald	7784-6.
1 Nilgiris	Dr. T. C. Jerdon	7787.
1 Pegu?	E. Gerard [P.]	12372.

247. DRYOPHIS DISPAR, Gunth.

Boulenger, p. 368.
Distribution—Anamalai Hills, South India.

2 Anamalais, S. Ind.	Col. R. H. Beddome	4396, 4407.

248. DRYOPHIS FRONTICINCTUS, (Gunth.).

Boulenger, p. 368; Sclater, J. A. S. B. lx, p. 244.
Distribution—Assam and Burma.

1 Sibsagar, Assam	S. E. Peal	6924.
2 Moulmein, Burma	F. Stoliczka [P.]	7791-2.

249. DRYOPHIS PRASINUS, Boie.

Boulenger, p. 369.
Distribution—Sikkim, Assam, Burma, Cochin China, Malay Peninsula and Islands.

1 Dacca	N. Belletty	8776.
2 Darjeeling	J. Gammie	7803-4.
1 Charapunji	J. H. Bourne	7793.
1 Duffla hills	Duffla Exped. (Godwin Austen)	4001.
1 Samaguting	Capt. J. Butler	7794
2 Naga hills	J. Gregory	8414-5.
1 Sibsagar	S. E. Peal	7824.
2 Cachar	Mus. Coll.	8416-7.
1 Sylhet	F. Skipwith	7790.
1 Chittagong hill tracts	J. T. Jarbo	11415.
1 Pegu	No hist.	7795.
1 N. Tenasserim	Tenasserim Exped. (Limborg)	4075.
1 Moulmein	Capt. J. H. Hood	4108.
4 Tavoy	Mus. Coll.	12676, 12702-4.
1 Burma-Siam hills.	Mus. Coll.	12779
2 Elphinstone Isle, Mergui	Mergui Exped. (Anderson)	11576-7.
1 Kisseraing Isle, Mergui	Mergui Exped. (Anderson)	11575.
3 Mergui	Mergui Exped. (Anderson)	11578-9, 11581.
1 Mergui	Major Berdmore, A. S. B.	7789.

1 Pinang	R. W. G. Frith	7788.
2 Johore	J. Meldrum	4656, 8609.
3 Singapore	Capt. T. S. Gardiner	12808, 12810, 13405.
1 Singapore	Mus. Coll.	7905.
1 Sinkip Isle	Mus. Coll.	7906.
5 Dehli, Sumatra	L. Schwendler	11436, 11440, 11447, 11449, 11451.
1 Borneo	E. Gerard [P.]	12386.

250. DRYOPHIS MYCTERIZANS, (Daud.).

Boulenger, p. 370; Sclater, J. A. S. B. lx. p. 244.
Distribution—India, Ceylon, Assam and Burma.

1 Mt. Aboo, Rajpt.	G. S. Sutherland	8425.
1 Chanda C. P.	Mus. Coll.	7827.
1 Bangalore	E. A. Minchin	12954.
1 Madras	S. Ransom	11402.
2 Travancore	Trevandrum Museum	13500-1.
1 Galle, Ceylon	S. Ransom	11392.
1 Ceylon	J. Anderson	7817.
1 Manbhum	V. Ball	8862.
2 Manbhum	W. Swinhoe	8867-8.
1 Purneah	Purchased	10977.
3 Calcutta	Sir J. Fayrer	8860-1, 8863.
1 Calcutta	J. Wood Mason	8869.
1 Calcutta	E. Blyth, A. S. B.	7808.
4 Dhappa nr. Calcutta	J. F. Galiffe	7818, 8864-5, 8870.
1 Dhappa nr. Calcutta	E. Jackson	8871.
1 Mutlah	W. Swinhoe	8866.
1 Sundarbans	W. Swinhoe	8872.
1 Lower Bengal	No hist., A. S. B.	7809.
2 Bhamo	Yunan Exped. (Anderson)	7825-6.

251. DRYOPHIS PULVERULENTUS, (Dum. & Bibr.).

Boulenger, p. 371; Sclater, J. A. S. B. lx, p. 244.
Distribution—India and Ceylon.

1 South India	Col. R. H. Beddome	8386.
6 Manbhum	V. Ball	7811-6.

252. DRYOPHIS ACUMINATA, (Wied).

Günther Cat. Col. Snakes, p. 156.
Distribution—Tropical South America and the West Indies.

1 West Indies	G. E. Dobson [Ex.]	8772.

253. BUCEPHALUS CAPENSIS, Smith.

Günther, Cat. Col. Snakes, p. 143.
Distribution—South and East Africa.

1 Senafe Tigré, Abyssinia 8000 ft.	W. T. Blanford	3199.
1 No loc.	No history	8714.

254. CHRYSOPELEA ORNATA, (Shaw).

Boulenger, p. 371.

Distribution—Southern India and Ceylon, Bengal, Assam, Burma, S. China, Siam, Malay Peninsula and Islands.

1 Travancore	Trevandrum Museum	13503.
1 Calcutta	D. D. Cunningham	7776.
1 Garo hills, Assam	Capt. Williamson	7777.
1 Samaguting	Capt. J. Butler	7778.
1 Naga hills	Capt. H. Butcher	8775.
1 Nazira, Sibsagar dist.	J. M. Foster	7770.
1 Mandalay	Yunan Exped. (Anderson)	7750.
1 Mandalay	F. B. Sladen	7769.
1 Moulmein	Capt. I. H. Hood	4112.
1 Shwegyen dist.	Major Berdmore	7760.
1 Semudaing, Tavoy	Mus. Coll.	12818.
1 Mergui	Mergui Exped. (Anderson)	11573.
1 Burma	F. Stoliczka	7774.
1 Burma	B. Powell	8470.
1 India	Rev. H. J. Harrison	8356.
3 Penang	F. Stoliczka	7762, 7765, 7771.
2 Malacca	Rev. E. Lindstedt	7755-6.
2 Johore	J. Meldrum	7748-9.
1 Johore	Mus. Coll.	7892.
1 Singapore	Derrick Spon	12960.
1 Singapore	Raffles Mus. (Davison)	13319.
1 Hongkong	Hongkong Mus. [Ex.]	12694.
1 No loc.	Sir J. Fayrer	7779.
2 No loc.	No hist., A. S. B.	7751, 7761.
4 No loc.	No hist.	7767-8, 7772-3.

255. CHRYSOPELEA RUBESCENS, (Gray).

Günther, Reptiles Brit. Ind., p. 299.

Distribution—Malay Peninsula, Sumatra, Borneo and Philippines.

1 Penang hill	F. Stoliczka [P.]	7780.

Subfamily HOMALOPSINAE.

256. HOMALOPSIS BUCCATA, (Linn.).

Boulenger, p. 374.

Distribution—Burma, Siam, Cambodia, Malay Peninsula and Islands.

1 Martaban	Major Berdmore, A. S. B.	8137.
	(TYPE OF H. SEMIZONATA, Bly.).	
1 Moulmein dist.	Capt. I. H. Hood	8138.
1 Johore	J. Meldrum	8742.
1 Johore	Mus. Coll.	7893.
1 Siam	Hongkong Mus. [Ex.]	12691.

257. CERBERUS RHYNCHOPS, (Schneid.).

Boulenger, p. 374; Sclater, J. A. S. B. lx, p. 244.
Distribution—India, Ceylon, Burma, Andamans, Malay Peninsula and Islands to New Guinea and N. Australia.

1 Galle, Ceylon	J. Anderson	8105.
1 Cocanada	W. T. Blanford	8106.
1 Barrakur, Burdwan dist.	G. Nevill	8107.
26 Botanical Gardens, Calcutta	J. Anderson	8111-36.
1 Salt Water Lakes, Calcutta	Sir J. Fayrer	8108.
1 Calcutta	L. Schwendler	8419.
1 Sundarbans	Genl. A. A. A. Kinloch	11407.
4 Lower Bengal	No hist., A. S. B.	8095-6, 8100, 8102.
1 Elephant Pt., Rangoon	J. Armstrong	8599.
1 Moulmein	Dr. Mason, A. S. B.	8101.
1 Amherst	F. Stoliczka [P.]	8103.
2 Mergui	Mergui Exped. (Anderson)	11552-3.
2 Andamans	Col. R. C. Tytler	8092, 8094.
1 Andamans	Capt. Hodge	8093.
1 Andamans	Capt. Rogers	8104.
1 South Andamans	J. Wood-Mason	4499.
1 Nicobars	F. A. de Roepstorf.	12541.
1 Johore	Mus. Coll.	7894.
3 Singapore	Capt. T. S. Gardiner	13162, 12641, 13289.
1 Malay Peninsula	Raffles Museum	13316.
1 No loc.	No. hist.	8418.

258. HYPSIRHINA PLUMBEA, (Boie).

Boulenger, p. 376.
Distribution—Burma, South China, Indo-China, Malay Peninsula and Islands.

1 Irrawaddy R. at Mandalay	F. Stoliczka [P.]	8193.
7 No loc.	No history, A. S. B.	8181-4, 8191-2, 8187.

259. HYPSIRHINA ENHYDRIS, (Schneid.).

Boulenger, p. 376.
Distribution—S. India, Ceylon, Bengal, Assam, Burma, Southern China, Indo-China, Malay Peninsula and Islands.

1 Govindpur, Manbhum dist.	E. V. Westmacott	8149.
3 Manbhum	Mus. Coll.	8146-8.
1 Darbhangah	C. Maries	11935.
1 Calcutta	Sir J. Fayrer	8175.
3 Calcutta	C. Swaries	8139, 8142, 8144.
14 Ooluberiah, Howrah dist.	J. Anderson	8151-63, 8176.
1 Sundarbans	W. Swinhoe	8179.
2 Kendrapara, Orissa	A. J. Fraser	13201-2.
1 Goalpara	H. L. Haughton	8150.
1 Cachar	Mus. Coll.	8164.
1 Sagain; nr. Mandalay	Yunan Exped. (Anderson)	8691.
2 Tavoy	Mergui Exped. (Anderson)	11586-7.

260. HYPSIRHINA BLANFORDI, Boul.

Boulenger, p. 377; Sclater, J. A. S. B. lx, p. 244.
Distribution—Burma.

1 Burma?	No hist.	8207.

(TYPE H. MACULATA, Blanford*).

261. HYPSIRHINA SIEBOLDII, (Schleg.).

Boulenger, p. 377; Sclater, J. A. S. B. lx, p. 245.
Distribution—India, Assam, Burma and the Malay Peninsula.

1 Jumna R. at Agra	Agra Museum	8198.
(TYPE OF FERANOIDES JAMNAETICA, Carlleyle).		
2 Monghyr	E. Lockwood	8576-7.
1 Samaguting	Capt. J. Butler	8199.
1 Pegu	Major Berdmore A. S. B.	8197.

262. HYPSIRHINA BENNETTI, Gray.

Gray, Cat. Snakes, B. M. p. 74.

1 Formosa	Hongkong Mus. [Ex.]	12693.

263. FORDONIA LEUCOBALIA, (Schleg.).

Boulenger, p. 378; Sclater, J. A. S. B. lx, p. 245.
Distribution—Lower Bengal, Burma, Nicobars, Malay Peninsula and Islands as far as Australia.

1 Sundarbans	Rev. H. J. Harrison	8441.
1 Singapore	Capt. T. S. Gardiner	12805.
1 Singapore	Raffles Mus. (Davison)	13314.
2 No loc.	No hist., A. S. B.	8155-6.
1 No loc.	No hist.	8741.

264. GERARDIA PREVOSTIANA, (Eyd. & Gerv.).

Boulenger, p. 379.
Distribution—Burma.

5 Pegu?	F. Stoliczka	8373-7.
1 Amherst, Tenasserim	J. Armstrong	8421.
2 No loc.	No hist., A. S. B.	8188-9.

265. CANTORIA VIOLACEA, Girard.

Boulenger, p. 380.
Distribution—Tenasserim, Malay Peninsula and Borneo.

1 Amherst, Tenasserim	F. Stoliczka.	8195.
(TYPE OF C. DAYANA, Stol.).		
1 Singapore	Raffles Mus. (Davison)	13315.

* The specific name blanfordi was substituted by Boulenger as maculata is preoccupied.

266. HIPISTES HYDRINUS, (Cantor).

Boulenger, p. 382.
Distribution—Coasts of Burma and Malay Peninsula.

1 Rangoon	Sir J. Fayrer, A. S. B.	8200.
2 Elephant pt., Rangoon.	J. Armstrong	8433-4.
4 Amherst	F. Day	8201-4.
2 Amherst ?	F. Stoliczka	8205-6.
1 Mergui	Mergui Exped. (Anderson)	11551.
1 King Isle, Mergui	Mergui Exped. (Anderson)	11856.

Subfamily ELAPINAE.

267. CALLOPHIS TRIMACULATUS, (Daud.).

Boulenger, p. 384.
Distribution—Southern India, Tenasserim and Bengal ?

1 Travancore	Col. R. H. Beddome	4439.

268. CALLOPHIS MACULICEPS, (Gunth.).

Boulenger, p. 384.
Distribution—Burma, Cochin China and Malay Peninsula.

3 Rangoon	Sir J. Fayrer, A. S. B.	2937-9.
1 Rangoon	W. Theobald	2948.
1 Amherst, Tenasserim	E. O' Reilly, A. S. B.	2940.

269. CALLOPHIS NIGRESCENS, Gunth.

Boulenger, p. 384; Sclater J. A. S. B. lx, p. 245.
Distribution—Hills of South India extending north to Ganjam.

1 Wynāad	Col. R. H. Beddome	2946.
1 Malabar	Col. R. H. Beddome	4420.
1 Malabar	E. Gerard [P.]	12365.
1 Anamalai hills	Col. R. H. Beddome	4416.
1 Shevaroy hills, Salem dist.	Col. R. H. Beddome	2949.
1 Ganjam	Col. R. H. Beddome	8442.

270. CALLOPHIS MACLELLANDI, (Reinh.).

Boulenger, p. 384.
Distribution—Nepal, Sikkim, Assam, Burma and Southern China.

1 Katmandn, Nepal	Dr. H. Whitwell	8771.
1 Darjeeling	J. Gammie	2944.
1 Shillong, Assam	Dr. G. M. Giles	13408.
1 Sibsagar	S. E. Peal	4041.
1 Samaguting	Capt. J. Butler	2945.
1 Assam	W. Robinson, A. S. B.	2933.
3 Pegu	Major Berdmore A. S. B.	2934-6.
1 Hongkong	Hongkong Mus. [Ex.]	12698.
1 No loc.	No history	8695.

271. CALLOPHIS BIBRONI, (Jan).

Boulenger, p. 386.
Distribution—The Wynaad in Southern India.

1 South India	Col. R. H. Beddome	11376.

272. CALLOPHIS GRACILIS, Gray.

Günther, Reptiles Brit. Ind., p. 349.
Distribution—Malay Peninsula.

1 Johore	Raffles Mus. (Davison)	13323.

273. ADENOPHIS BIVIRGATUS, (Boie).

Günther, Reptiles Brit. Ind. p. 348.
Distribution—Malay Peninsula, Sumatra, Java and Borneo.

2 Singapore	Mus. Coll.	7907-8.
1 Sinkip Isle, Sumatra	J. Wood-Mason	8420.
1 Borneo	Raffles Mus. (Davison)	13322.

274. ADENOPHIS INTESTINALIS, (Laur.).

Boulenger, p. 386.
Distribution—Burma, Malay Peninsula, Sumatra, Java, Borneo, and the Philippines.

1 Upper Burma	F. Stoliczka	2947.
1 Perak	Mus. Coll.	13251.
1 Johore	J. Meldrum	4659.
1 Johore	Mus. Coll.	4239.
2 Singapore	R. W. G. Frith, A. S. B.	2941.
1 Singapore	Raffles Mus. (Davison)	13330.

275. MEGAEROPHIS FLAVICEPS, (Reinh.).

Günther, Reptiles Brit. Ind. p. 346; Sclater, J. A. S. B. lx, p. 245.
Distribution—Mergui, Malay Peninsula, Sumatra, Java and Borneo.

1 Mergui	W. Theobald, A. S. B.	2932.

276. BUNGARUS FASCIATUS, (Schneid.).

Boulenger, p. 388.
Distribution—Bengal and Southern India, Assam, Burma, South China, Indo-China, Malay Peninsula, Sumatra and Java.

1 Aska, Ganjam dist.	E. A. Minchin	12950.
1 Raniganj, Burdwan dist.	Purchased	2933.
1 Botanical Gardens, Calcutta	J. Anderson	2931.
1 Dacca	Mus. Coll.	2926.
1 Sibsagar, Assam	S. E. Peal	2922.
1 Samaguting, Assam	Capt. J. Butler	2928.

1 Cachar	O. L. Fraser	13281.
1 Mandalay	F. B. Sladen	2929.
1 Sagain nr. Mandalay	Yunan Exped. (Anderson)	8740.
2 Johore, Malay P.	J. Meldrum	4650-1.
1 No loc.	No hist.	2920.

277. BUNGARUS CEYLONICUS, Gunth.

Boulenger, p. 288.
Distribution—Ceylon and South India ?

1 near Kandy, Ceylon	W. Ferguson	2915.
1 Ceylon	E. Gerard [P.]	12398.

278. BUNGARUS CAERULEUS, (Schneid.).

Boulenger, p. 388 ; Sclater, J. A. S. B. lx, p. 245.
Distribution— Throughout India from the Punjab to Tinnevelli, Burma ?

1 Rajanpur, Pjb.	Dr. E. Sanders	2907.
1 Jaipur, Rjpt.	R. Pattoon	3217.
4 Agra	Agra Mns.	2908-9, 2911-2.
1 Allahabad	J. Cockburn	8731.
1 Bilaspur, C. P.	W. T. Blanford	2899.
1 Tinnevelli hills	Col. R. H. Beddome	7577.
2 Aska, Ganjam dist.	E. A. Minchin	12948-9.
2 Darbhangah	C. Maries	11929-30.
1 Godda, Sonthal Pg.	J. A. Craven	11998.
1 Govindpur, Manbhum dist.	E. V. Westmacott	2902.
1 Raniganj	Purchased	2904.
1 Serampore, Hugli dist.	Genl. G. B. Mainwaring	2906.
1 Rangoon	Col. Nuthall, A. S. B.	2891.
2 Meiktila, Shan hills	Genl. H. Collett.	13244-5.
1 "Cape of Good Hope"	Col. R. C. Tytler	2897.

279. BUNGARUS BUNGAROIDES (Cantor).

Boulenger, p. 389 ; Sclater, J. A. S. B. lx, p. 246.
Distribution—Sikkim and Khasia hills.

1 Darjeeling	W. S. Atkinson	2898.
2 Darjeeling	J. Gammie	7741-2.
1 Labdah nr. Kurseong	J. L. Lister	8692.

280. BUNGARUS LIVIDUS, (Cantor).

Boulenger, p. 390 ; Sclater, J. A. S. B. lx, p. 246.
Distribution—Northern Bengal and Assam.

1 Saidpur, Dinagepur dist.	W. de W. Peal	11419.
1 Garo hills	Capt. Williamson	3941.
1 Sibsagar	S. E. Peal.	4013.

281. BUNGARUS SEMIFASCIATUS, Kuhl.

Günther, Reptiles Brit. Ind. p. 344.
Distribution—Southern China and Formosa.

1 Hongkong	Dr. R. Hungerford	11948.
1 Hongkong	Hongkong Mus. [Ex.]	12695.

282. NAIA TRIPUDIANS, Merr.

Boulenger, p. 392; Sclater, J. A. S. B. lx, p. 246.

Distribution—From the Eastern shores of the Caspian sea eastwards, throughout India, Ceylon, Assam, Burma, Andamans, South China, Indo-China, Malay Peninsula and Sumatra.

1 Simla	F. Stoliczka	8324.
1 Khojak, Bt. Baluchistan	J. A. Murray	11422.
2 Rajanpur, Pjb.	Dr. E. Sanders	8354, 8733.
1 Hissar, Pjb.	Col. J. A. McMahon	8768.
1 Bakadra, Jaisalmir	N. Belletty	13381.
1 Jaipur	R. Pattoon	3206.
1 Matourah, Banda dist., N. W. P.	J. Cockburn	11454.
1 Ceylon	W. Ferguson	8343.
1 Aska, Ganjam dist.	E. A. Minchin	12953.
1 Assensole	G. A. Apcar	12874.
2 Calcutta	Sir J. Fayrer	8334, 8336.
4 Calcutta	Purchased	12590-3.
3 Dhappa nr. Calcutta	J. F. Galiffe	8338-40.
1 Salt Water Lakes, Calcutta	J. F. Galiffe	8912.
1 Alipore	Sir J. Fayrer	8330.
1 Botanical Gardens, Calcutta	J. Anderson	8781.
1 Sundarbans	J. F. Barcklay	4133.
1 Krishnagarh	R. de Dombal	8329.
2 Kaliganj, Rungpur dist.	W. Dodgson	8325-6.
2 Sibsagar, Assam	S. E. Peal	4011-2.
1 Samaguting	Capt. J. Butler	8327.
1 Assam	No history	8353.
1 Chittagong	B. Macdonald	7884.
1 Chittagong hill tracts	J. T. Jarbo	11413.
1 Mandalay	Yunan Exped. (Anderson)	8346.
2 Mandalay	Capt. F. B. Sladen	8332, 8341.
1 Pagan, Burma	Yunan Exped. (Anderson)	8328.
1 Meiktila, Shan hills	Gen. H. Collett	13243.
1 Mergui	W. Theobald, A. S. B.	8312.
1 Port Blair, Andamans	Major Ford	8342.
1 Andamans	V. Ball	8321.
5 Singapore	Capt. T. S. Gardiner	13148, 13166, 13289, 13400, 13406.
4 Singapore	Mr. Derrick Spon	12956-9.
1 Deli, Sumatra	L. Schwendler	11435.
1 Hongkong	Dr. R. Hungerford	11949.
1 Hongkong	Hongkong Museum [Ex.]	12690.
1 (double-headed)	Nawab of Dacca, A. S. B.	8319.
23 (Eggs)	No history	8322-3, 8347-9. 8751.

283. NAIA BUNGARUS, Schleg.

Boulenger, p. 393.

Distribution—The Himalayas and throughout India, Assam, Burma and the Andamans, Siam, the Malay Peninsula, Java, Borneo, Sumatra and the Philippines.

1 Mussooree	Mrs. Moss	12556.
2 Darjeeling	J. Gammie	8294, 8823.

1 Nagasurie, Jalpi. dist.	G. W. Shillingford	12877.
1 Botanical Gardens, Calcutta	J. Anderson	8292.
1 Samaguting	Capt. J. Butler	8754.
1 Andamans	Capt. Rogers	8293.
1 No loc.	No hist.	8295.

284. DIEMENIA OLIVACEA, Gray.

Krefft, Austr. Snakes, p. 39.
Distribution—North-Eastern parts of Australia.

1 Queensland	Brisbane Mus.	11875.

285. DIEMENIA RETICULATA, Gray.

Krefft, Austr. Snakes, p. 40.
Distribution—Throughout Australia.

1 Australia	E. Gerard [P.]	12366

286. PSEUDECHIS PORPHYRIACUS, (Shaw).

Krefft, Austr. Snakes, p. 46.
Distribution—Throughout Australia.

1 Queensland	Brisbane Mus. [Ex.]	11874.
1 Australia	G. E. Dobson	8771.
1 Australia	E. Gerard [P.]	12367.

287. BRACHYSOMA DIADEMA, (Schleg.).

Krefft, Austr. Snakes, p. 48.
Distribution—Australia north of the Murray River.

1 Australia	E. Gerard [P.]	12389.

288. HOPLOCEPHALUS GOULDII, (Gray).

Krefft, Austr. Snakes, p. 60.
Distribution—Australia.

2 Queensland	Brisbane Mus. [Ex.]	1186-7.

289. CACOPHIS HARRIETAE, Krefft.

Krefft, Austr. Snakes, p. 76.
Distribution—Queensland.

1 Queensland	Brisbane Mus. [Ex.]	11868.

290. ACANTHOPHIS ANTARCTICUS, Wagler.

Krefft, Austr. Snakes, p. 80.
Distribution—Australia except in the extreme south.

1 Brisbane dist.	Brisbane Museum [Ex.]	11873.
1 Queensland	Brisbane Museum [Ex.]	11877.

1 N. S. Wales	Calcutta Exhibition	12624.
1 N. S. Wales	G. Nevill	12033.

291. ELAPS FULVIUS, (Linn.).

Garman, N. Amer. Snakes, p. 105.
Distribution—Southern United States and Mexico.

1 S. Antonio, Texas, U. S. A.	Dr. J. H. Garnier [Ex.]	12263.
1 Louisiana, U. S. A.	Dr. J. H. Garnier [Ex.]	12168.

292. ELAPS NIGROCINCTUS, Girard.

Cope, Proceed. Acad. Nat. Sci. Philad., 1859, p. 345.
Distribution—Central America.

2 Guatemala	Brit. Mus. [Ex.]	4746-7.
1 Costa Rica	E. Gerard [P.]	12370.

293. ELAPS LEMNISCATUS, (Linn.).

Günther, Cat. Col. Snakes, p. 234.
Distribution—Tropical South America.

1 Bahia	British Mus. [Ex.]	4748.
1 Brazil	E. Gerard [P.]	12363.

294. ELAPS HYGIAE, (Shaw).

Günther, Cat. Col. Snakes, p. 232.
Distribution—South Africa.

1 S. Africa	Dr. Withecomb, A. S. B.	2942.
1 S. Africa	Netley Mus. [Ex.]	8640.

295. VERMICELLA ANNULATA, Gunth.

Krefft, Austr. Snakes, p. 78.
Distribution—Throughout Australia.

1 Logan, Queensland	Brisbane Mus. [Ex.]	11879.
4 Queensland	Brisbane Mus. [Ex.]	11878, 11880-2.
1 N. S. Wales	G. Nevill	12035.

Subfamily HYDROPHIINAE.

296. PLATURUS LATICAUDATUS, (Linn.).

Boulenger, p. 395.
Distribution—Bay of Bengal and Chinese Seas to Polynesia.

1* Tolly's Nullah, Calcutta	Sir J. Fayrer	8289.
1 Penang	Capt. Lewis, A. S. B.	8286.

* Figured by Fayrer, Thanatophidia, pl. XIX.

297. PLATURUS COLUBRINUS, (Schneid.).

Boulenger, p. 395.
Distribution—Bay of Bengal, Chinese and Australian seas.

1 Ramri Isle, Arakan	Capt. Abbott, A. S. B.	8285.
1 Nicobars	J. Wood-Mason	8287.
1 Nicobars	F. A. de Roepstorf	8288.
1 New South Wales	Calcutta Exhibition	12625.

298. ENHYDRIS CURTUS, (Shaw).

Boulenger, p. 396.
Distribution—Coasts of India and Ceylon.

1* Puri, Orissa	Sir J. Fayrer	8241.

299. ENHYDRIS HARDWICKII, (Gray).

Boulenger, p. 397.
Distribution—Bay of Bengal, Chinese and Malayan seas to New Guinea.

1 Puri, Orissa	Sir J. Fayrer	8270.
	(TYPE OF HYDROPHIS FAYRERIANA, Anders.).	
10 Mergui	Mergui Exped. (Anderson)	11504, 11528-32. 11535, 11537-9.
2 Fishing Stakes, 7 miles from Mergui	Mergui Exped. (Anderson)	11533, 11536.

300. HYDRUS PLATURUS, (Linn.).

Boulenger, p. 397.
Distribution—Throughout the Indian, and Tropical parts of the Pacific Oceans.

1 Persian Gulf at Gwadar	Persian Coll. (Blanford)	8467.
1 Calachal, S. Travancore	R. B. Foote	11946.
1 Columbo harbour	Marine Survey (Giles)	13090.
1 Aripo, W. Coast of Ceylon	W. Ferguson	8282.
1 Ceylon	F. Stoliczka	8284.
1† Puri, Orissa	Sir J. Fayrer	8283.
1 Nicobars	M. Bunsch, A. S. B.	8281.
1 Bay of Bengal	J. H. T. Walsh	13394.

301. HYDROPHIS CAERULESCENS, (Shaw).

Boulenger, p. 400.
Distribution—Coasts of India and Burma as far as Malacca.

1 Sandheads, Hugli R.	C. J. Scott	8413.
1 Sandheads, Hugli R.	Messrs. Rust and Elson	13246.
2 Sandheads, Hugli R.	J. Lark	13158, 13160.

* Figured by Fayrer, Thanatophidia, pl. XXIV.
† Figured by Fayrer, Thanatophidia, pl. XVII.

1 Sandheads, Hugli R.	A. S. B.	8233.
2 Fishing Stakes, 7 miles from Mergui	Mergui Exped. (Anderson)	11483, 11500.

302. HYDROPHIS NIGROCINCTUS, Daud.

Boulenger, p. 400.
Distribution—Bay of Bengal extending to the Straits of Malacca.

2 No loc.	No hist.	8239-40.

303. HYDROPHIS LATIFASCIATUS, Gunth.

Boulenger, p. 401.
Distribution—Coasts of India and Burma from Sind to Mergui.

1 Mergui	Mergui Exped. (Anderson)	11496.

304. HYDROPHIS CORONATUS, Gunth.

Boulenger, p. 402.
Distribution—Coasts of Bengal and mouth of the Hugli.

1 Tolly's Nullah, Calcutta	Sir J. Fayrer	8773.
1 Hugli R. at Botanical Gardens	J. Anderson	8234.
1 Hugli R.	J. Anderson	8255.
1 Hijili, mouth of Hugli	H. L. Haughton	8253.
1 Sundarbans	Capt. H. Butcher	8522.

305. HYDROPHIS OBSCURUS, Daud.

Boulenger, p. 403.
Distribution—Bay of Bengal.

1 Hugli R.	J. Anderson	8262.
1 Hugli R. at Hijili	H. L. Haughton, A. S. B.	8256.
1 Elephant Pt., nr. Rangoon	J. Armstrong	8598.
1 Mergui	J. Anderson	11499.
1 Fishing Stakes 7 miles from Mergui	Mergui Exped. (Anderson)	11498.
1 No loc.	No hist.	8254.

306. HYDROPHIS FASCIATUS, (Schneid.).

Boulenger, p. 404.
Distribution—Coasts of India to Siam and the Malay Archipelego.

3 Puri	Sir J. Fayrer	8261, 8264-5.
2 Sandheads, Hugli R.	No hist., A. B. S.	8258-9.
1 Akyab	A. Dunn, A. S. B.	8257.
1 Bay of Bengal	J. H. T. Walsh	13393.

307. HYDROPHIS GRACILIS, (Shaw).

Boulenger, p. 404.

Distribution—Persian Gulf, Coasts of India and Burma to the Malay Archipelego.

1 Persian Gulf at Gwadar	Persian Coll. (Blanford)	8468.
2 Karachi	Karachi Mus. [Ex.]	8543-4.
1 Puri, Orissa	Sir J. Fayrer	8236.
1 Puri, Orissa	Marine Survey (Alcock)	13276.
1 Hugli R. at Hijili	H. L. Haughton, A. S. B.	8268.
1 Mergui	Mergui Exped. (Anderson)	11484.

308. HYDROPHIS CANTORIS, Gunth.

Boulenger, p. 405.

Distribution—Bay of Bengal to the Straits of Malacca.

2 Puri, Orissa	Sir J. Fayrer	8263, 8627.
1 Puri	Commr. of Puri	12098.
1 Sandheads, Hugli R.	W. Earl, A. S. B.	8232.
1 Sandheads	Sir J. Fayrer	8260.
1 Sandheads	J. Barnett	12853.
1 Sandheads	Purchased	8231.
1 Saugor Roads, Hugli R.	S. Elson	12587.
1 Indian seas	F. Stoliczka	8623.

309. HYDROPHIS ELEGANS. (Gray).

Günther, Reptiles Brit. Ind., p. 369.

Distribution—Coasts of Australia.

1 No loc.	Brit. Mus. [Ex.]	4751.

310. ENHYDRINA VALAKADIEN, (Boie).

Boulenger, p. 406.

Distribution—Coasts of South-East Asia from the Persian Gulf to New Guinea.

1 Persian Gulf at Gwadar	Persian Coll. (Blanford)	4611.
2 Karachi harbour	Capt. Russell	8517, 8689.
1 Karachi	Karachi Mus. [Ex.]	8409.
2 Off Cannanore, Malabar Coast	F. Grieves	13156-7.
1 Gopalpore, Ganjam dist.	Purchased	8230.
1 Puri, Orissa	Sir J. Fayrer	8228.
1 Near Puri	Marine Survey (Alcock)	13275.
1 Orissa	Purchased	8220.
1 Tolly's Nullah, Calcutta	Sir J. Fayrer	8934.
1 Hugli R.	F. Stoliczka	8624.
1 Hugli R.	Capt. T. S. Gardiner	13168.
1 Sandheads, Hugli R.	C. J. Scott	8528.
1 Sandheads	A. Milne	12716.
1 Sandheads	J. Lark	13159.
1 Sandheads	Messrs. Rust and Elson	13247.
1 Hijili, Hugli R.	H. L. Haughton, A. S. B.	8222.
1 Saugor Isle, Hugli Mouth	S. R. Elson	12036.

3 30 M. S. of Saugor	C. Mills	11954-5, 11957.
1 Phool Malenchow R. Sunderbans	O. L. Fraser	8721.
1 60 M. from Chittagong	Marine Survey (Giles)	13091.
1 Elephant Pt., Rangoon	J. Armstrong	8597.
1 Entrance of Ye R., Tenasserim	Marine Survey (Giles)	13092.
1 Bay of Bengal	J. Anderson	8621.
17 Mergui	Mergui Exped. (Anderson)	11501, 11506-7, 11509, 11510, 11513-20, 11522-4, 11527.
1 Fishing Stakes, 7 miles from Mergui	Mergui Exped. (Anderson)	11512.

311. DISTIRA JERDONI, (Gray).

Boulenger, p. 407.
Distribution—Bay of Bengal to the Straits of Malacca.

1 Off Madras	F. Grieves	13188.
1* Puri, Orissa	Sir J. Fayrer	8280.
1 Mergui	W. Theobald, A. S. B.	8237.
4 Mergui	Mergui Exped. (Anderson)	11486-9.

312. DISTIRA ROBUSTA, (Gunth.).

Boulenger, p. 409.
Distribution—Coasts of India from the Persian Gulf to Singapore.

1 Off Cuddalore, S. Arcot. dist.	F. Grieves	13155.
7 Ganjam	Mus. Coll.	12914-20.
4 Puri	Sir J. Fayrer	8243-5, 8273.
1 Hijili, Hugli Mouth	H. L. Haughton	8252.
2 Mergui	Mergui Exped. (Anderson)	11485, 11505.
1 Singapore	Raffles Mus. (Davison)	13324.

313. DISTIRA TUBERCULATA, (Anders.).

Boulenger, p. 409.
Distribution—Tidal streams, Calcutta.

1 Canal at Dhappa, Calcutta	J. F. Galiffe	8271.

(TYPE OF HYDROPHIS TUBERCULATA, Anderson).

314. DISTIRA CYANOCINCTA, (Daud.).

Boulenger, p. 410; Sclater, J. A. S. B. lx, p. 247.
Distribution—Coasts of India, China and Japan.

3 Karachi	Karachi Mus. [Ex.]	8408, 8410-1.
1 Puri	Sir J. Fayrer	8249.
1† Hugli below Calcutta	J. Anderson	8272.

(TYPE OF HYDROPHIS CRASSICOLLAS, Anders.).

* Figured by Fayrer, Thanatophidia, pl. XX.
† Figured by Fayrer, Thanatophidia, pl. XXII.

2 Sandheads, Hugli Mouth	Sir J. Fayrer	8250-1.
1 Hijili at Hugli Mouth	H. L. Haughton, A. S. B.	8247.
2 Mergui	W. Theobald, A. S. B.	8266-7.

(TYPES OF HYDROPHIS TRACHYCEPS, Theobald).

6 Mergui	Mergui Exped. (Anderson)	11491-5, 11503.
1 China	C. J. Browning, A. S. B.	8246.
1 No loc.	No hist., A. S. B.	8242.
1 No loc.	No hist., A. S. B.	8248.

315. DISTIRA LAPEMIDOIDES, (Gray).

Boulenger, p. 312.
Distribution—Persian Gulf, Coasts of India and Ceylon.

1 Persian Gulf at Gwadar	Persian Coll. (Blanford)	8632.
1 Karachi	F. Stoliczka	8278.

(TYPE OF HYDROPHIS DAYANUS, Stoliczka).

1 Rangoon	Col. Nuthall, A. S. B.	8269.
1 Bay of Bengal	J. H. T. Walsh	13392.
1 No loo.	No hist.	8235.

316. DISTIRA VIPERINA, (Schmidt).

Boulenger, p. 413.
Distribution—Persian Gulf, Coasts of India and Burma to Southern China.

1 Muscat, Persian Gulf	Sheik Hinghoo Khan	8279.
4 Puri	Sir J. Fayrer	8274-7.
1 Mergui	Mergui Exped. (Anderson)	11497.

Family AMBLYCEPHALIDAE.

317. AMBLYCEPHALUS MONTICOLA, (Cantor).

Boulenger, p. 415; Sclater, J. A. S. B. lx, p. 247.
Distribution—Sikkim, Assam and the Nicobars.

1 Darjeeling	J. Gammie	8030.
1 Charapunji, Assam	J. H. Bourne	8648.
1 Charapunji, Assam	Col. H. H. Godwin Austen	8027.
2 Samaguting	Capt. J. Butler	8019-20.
2 Sibsagar	S. E. Peal	4028-9.
1 Camorta, Nicobars	F. A. de Roepstorf	8888.

318. AMBLYCEPHELUS MODESTUS, (Theob.).

Boulenger, p. 416.
Distribution—Burma.

1 Rangoon	Col. Nuthall	8028.

(TYPE OF PAREAS MODESTUS, Theobald).

319. AMBLYCEPHALUS MACULARIUS, (Theob.).

Boulenger, p. 416; Sclater, J. A. S. B. lx, p. 248.
Distribution—Tenasserim.

3 Martaban	Major Berdmore, A. S. B.	8024-6.

(TYPES OF PAREAS MACULARIUS, Theob.).

320. AMBLYCEPHALUS CARINATUS, (Reinw.).

Günther, Reptiles Brit. Ind. p. 248; Sclater, J. A. S. B. lx, p. 248.
Distribution—Tenasserim, Siam, Sumatra and Java.

3 Tenasserim	Major Berdmore, A. S. B.	8021-3.

(TYPES OF PAREAS BERDMOREI, Theob.).

2 Tavoy	Mus. Collector	12700-1.
1 Burma-Siam hills	Mus. Coll.	12781.
1 Sullivan Isle, Mergui	Mergui Exped. (Anderson)	11574.
1 Dehli, Sumatra	L. Schwendler	11434.

321. AMBLYCEPHALUS MOELLENDORFFII (Boettg.).

Boettger, Bericht Offenb. Ver. xxiv—xxv, p. 125.
Distribution—Tenasserim, Siam and South China.

1 Tenasserim	Tenasserim Exped. (Limborg)	4870.

322. LEPTOGNATHUS NEBULATUS, (Linn.).

Günther, Cat. Col. Snakes, p. 176.
Distribution—Mexico and the West Indies to Brazil.

1 British Guiana	British Mus. [Ex.]	4750.

Family VIPERIDAE.

Subfamily VIPERINAE.

323. VIPERA RUSSELLII, (Shaw).

Boulenger, p. 420.
Distribution—Himalayas, throughout India, Ceylon, Burma and Siam.

1 Kulu, Himalayas	F. Stoliczka	3157.
1 Travancore	Trevandrum Museum	13499.
1 Purneah, Bengal	W. Shillingford	3156.
1 Serampore, Hugli dist.	Gen. B. Mainwaring	8518.
1 Serampore, Hugli dist.	T. R. Doucett	8060.
3 Botanical, Gardens	J. Anderson	3152, 3155, 3158.
1 Tengra near Calcutta	R. D'Cruz	11391.
1 Ceylon	E. F. Kelaart, A. S. B.	3102.
1 Pagan, Upper Burma	Yunan Exped. (Anderson)	3153.
1 Rangoon	Rev. W. Whittaker	3111.

16 [Young of above taken out of the mother]	Rev. W. Whittaker	8487-502.
40 [Young from one mother]	Rev. W. Whittaker	3112-51.
2 India	Rev. H. L. Harrison	3109-10.

324. VIPERA LEBETINA, (Linn.).

Boulenger, p. 421.
Distribution—Northern Africa and Western Asia, extending to Afghanistan and Kashmir.

1 Niriz, Shiraz	Persian Coll. (Blanford)	3488.
1 Sang Kotal	Afghan B. Comm. (Aichison)	13137.
1 Kashmir	Yarkand Exped. (Stoliczka)	8628.

325. VIPERA AMMODYTES, (Linn.).

Schreiber, Herp. Europ., p. 187.
Distribution—Southern Europe and Western Asia.

2 Europe	Hungarian Mus. [Ex.]	3173-4.

326. PELIAS BERUS, (Linn.).

Schreiber, Herp. Europ., p. 202.
Distribution—Thronghout Europe.

2 Cheshire, England	E. Blyth, A. S. B.	3775-6.
5 England	Messrs. Strickland and Hancock, A. S. B.	3177-81.
1 Norway	No history, A. S. B.	3182.
3 Europe	Hungarian Mus., A. S. B.	3183-5.
1 Europe	Netley Mus. [Ex.]	8629.

327. CERASTES HASSELQUISTI, Gray.

Gray, Cat. Snakes B. M., p. 28.
Distribution—Northern Africa.

1 Egypt	Netley Mus. [Ex.]	8700.

328. CERASTES PERSICUS, Dum. & Bibr.

Blanford, Persia, p. 429.
Distribution—Persia and Beluchistan.

1 Isfandak, Baluch.	Persian Coll. (Blanford)	3491.

329. CLOTHO ARIETANS, Gray.

Gray, Cat. Snakes B. M., p. 25.
Distribution—South Africa.

1 Africa	E. Gerard [P.]	12388.

330. ECHIS CARINATA, (Schneid.).

Boulenger, p. 422.
Distribution—North Africa, Western Asia and throughout the greater part of India where dry.

2 Zoulla, Annesley Bay	Abyssinian Exped. (Blanford)	3171-2.
1 Btw. Karman and Shiraz, Persia	Persian Coll. (Blanford)	4608.
2 Bushire, Persia	W. D. Cumming	13419-20.
2 Kalagan, Baluchistan	Persian Coll. (Blanford)	4607, 8581.
1 Saman, Dasht, Baluch.	Persian Coll. (Blanford)	8637.
1 Tirphul near Herat	Afghan Bound. Comm. (Aichison)	13105.
1 Rajanpur, Pjb.	Dr. E. Sanders	8644.
3 Salt Range, Pjb.	W. Theobald	3161-3.
1 Ajmere, Rjpt.	Sir O. B. C. St. John.	13491.
1 Patchia, Rjpt.	N. Belletty	13382.
3 Mt. Aboo, Rjpt.	Dr. Sutherland	3168-70.
2 Karachi	Karachi Mus. [Ex.]	3167, 8746.
1 Agra	Sir J. Fayrer	3164.
1 Allahabad	J. Cockburn	8527.
1 Nowgong, C. P.	F. J. Daley	13412.
1 Bangalore	Purchased	8645.
1 Ellore, Md. Pr.	W. T. Blanford	3166.
1 Singbhum	V. Ball	3165.
2 Rajmahal	Purchased	10983-4.
1 Upper India	India Mus., London	3163.

331. ATHERIS SQUAMATA, (Hallow).

Cope, Proc. Acad. Philad., 1862, p. 341.
Distribution—West Africa.

1 Fernando Po	British Mus. [Ex.]	4743.

Subfamily CROTALINAE.

332. ANCISTRODON HIMALAYANUS, (Gunth.).

Boulenger, p. 424.
Distribution—The Himalayas from Gilgit to Sikkim.

1 Gilgit	Col. Biddulph	8774.
1 Ladak	No history	3094.
1 Betw. Sonamurg, Kashmir and Kharbu Ladak	Yarkand Exped. (Stoliczka)	8573.
1 Kashmir	G. W. Strettel	12602.
1 Murree	Yarkand Exped. (Stoliczka)	8438.
1 Dharmsála at foot of glacier, 16,000 ft.	H. M. Clark	12875.
1 Near Simla	R. D. Oldham	13189.
1 Hampton Court, Mussooree	J. Wood-Mason	13248.
3 Naini Tal,	J. Cockburn	4062-4.
1 Allahabad ?	J. Cockburn	8453.

333. ANCISTRODON HYPNALE (Merr.).

Boulenger, p. 424.
Distribution—Hills of Southern India and Ceylon.

1 Koppa, Mysore	W. M. Daly	13537.
1 Malabar district	Col. R. H. Beddome	4433.
1 Anamalai hills	Col. R. H. Beddome	4434.
1 Travancore hills	Col. R. H. Beddome	7575.
2 Ceylon	J. Anderson	3097.
	(TYPES OF HYPNALE AFFINIS, Anders.).	
1 Ceylon	W. Ferguson	3095.
5 No loc.	F. Stoliczka	3958-9, 4053, 8654-5.
2 No loc.	Col. R. H. Beddome	4432, 8762.

334. ANCISTRODON PALLASII, (Gunth.).

Blanford, Persia, p. 430.
Distribution—Elburz Mountains, Persia.

2 Anan, Mazendaran, N. Persia	Persian Coll. (Blanford)	4606, 8582.

335. ANCISTRODON CONTORTRIX, (Linn.).

Garman, Snakes N. Amer., p. 120.
Distribution—Eastern half of North America.

1 N. Carolina, U. S. A.	Rev. F. Fitzgerald, A. S. B.	3090.
1 Tennessee, U. S. A.	Dr. J. H. Garnier, [Ex.]	12166.
1 No loc.	No hist., A. S. B.	3093.

336. TRIMERESURUS MONTICOLA, (Gunth.).

Boulenger, p. 426.
Distribution—Nepal, Sikkim, Assam, Burma and Malay Peninsula.

1 Katmandu, Nepal	Mus. Coll.	3066.
2 Darjeeling	W. T. Blanford, A. S. B.	3058-9.
2 Darjeeling	Genl. B. Mainwaring	3068-9.
8 Darjeeling	J. Gammie	3060-1, 3064-5, 7722-3, 8806, 8826.
1 Shillong, Assam	G. M. Giles	13407.
1 Charapunji	Col. H. H. Godwin Austen	3067.
1 Charapunji	J. H. Bourne	8558.
3 Hotha, Yunan	Yunan Exped. (Anderson)	3079-81.
1 West Hill, Penang,	F. Stoliczka [P.]	3082.
	(TYPE OF TRIMERESURUS CONVICTUS, Stol.).	

337. TRIMERESURUS STRIGATUS, Gray.

Boulenger, p. 427.
Distribution—Hills of Southern India.

1 Nilgiris	W. Theobald, A. S. B.	3071.
1 Nilgiris	T. C. Jerdon	3072.

1 Nilgiris	E. A. Minchin	12937.
1 Anamalais	E. Gerard [P.]	12376.

338. TRIMERESURUS JERDONII, Gunth.

Boulenger, p. 427.
Distribution—Assam and Western China.

1 Shillong, Assam	Major C. R. Cock	8422.

339. TRIMERESURUS, CANTORIS, (Bly.).

Boulenger, p. 428.
Distribution—Nicobars and Andamans. ?

1 Nicobars	Messrs. Lewis and Barbe, A. S. B.	2959.
	(TYPE OF T. CANTORIS, Blyth.).	
12 Nicobars	F. A. de Roepstorf	2961-3, 8448-9. 12544-6, 12596-9.
4 Nicobars	F. Stoliczka [P.]	2966-9.
1 Nicobars	Purchased	2982.
1 Andamans ?	J. Wood-Mason	8716.
1 No loc.	G. E. Dobson	8450.

340. TRIMERESURUS PURPUREOMACULATUS, (Gray).

Boulenger, p. 429; Sclater, J. A. S. B. lx, p. 248.
Distribution—Lower Bengal, Assam, Burma, Malay Peninsula and Preparis Isle.

1 Port Canning	W. Swinhoe	2978.
1 Sundarbans	W. P. Arnot	2976.
4 Lower Bengal	No hist., A. S. B.	2950-1, 2955-6.
	(TYPES OF TRIMERESURUS PORPHYRACEUS, Bly ?)	
1 Charapunji, Assam	J. H. Bourne	3020.
2 Garo hills	Capt. Williamson	3016-7.
1 Garo hills	Col. H. H. Godwin Austen	2975.
1 Naga hills	Lieut. J. Gregory	3036.
40 Samaguting, Assam	Capt. J. Butler	2989-94, 2997-3006, 3008-15, 3039-41, 3043-55.
1 Chittagong	B. Macdonald	7885.
1 Rungamutti, Chittagong Hill Tracts	J. T. Jarbo	8444.
1 Ponsee, Kakhyen hills	Yunan Exped. (Anderson)	4185.
1 Prome	A. Dunn	3035.
1 Elephant Pt., Rangoon	J. Armstrong	8596.
2 Moulmein	Capt. Hood	4109, 7339.
3 Moulmein	F. Stoliczka [P.]	2973, 3033-4.
1 Gregory Isle, Mergui	Mergui Exped. (Anderson)	13169.
1 Pilai, Mergui	Mergui Exped. (Anderson)	11562.
1 Singapore ?	Raffles Mus. (Davison)	13326.
3 Preparis Isle, B. of Bengal	F. Stoliczka	3076-8.
2 Singapore	Mr. Derrick Spon	12961-2.
1 Singapore	Raffles Mus. (Davison)	13325.
1 Java	F. Stoliczka [P.]	3031.

341. TRIMERESURUS GRAMINEUS, (Shaw).

Boulenger, p. 429; Sclater, J. A. S. B. lx, p. 248.

Distribution—Himalayas from Simla to Assam, Burma, Andamans, Nicobars, Southern China, Indo-China, Malay Peninsula and Archipelego.

(A.) TYPICAL VARIETY.

2 near Simla	F. Stoliczka	3188-9.
1 Darjeeling	Genl. B. Mainwaring	3187.
9 Darjeeling	J. Gammie	3025-6, 3032, 7724-7, 8480-1.
4 Nagasurie, Jalpi dist.	G. W. Shillingford	12665-6, 12880-1.
1 Garo hills, Assam	Capt. Williamson	3942.
2 Charapnnji	J. H. Bourne	3021-2.
2 Khasia hills	Col. H. H. Godwin Austen	3023-4.
2 Nazira, Sibsagar distr.	J. M. Foster	3018-9.
12 Sibsagar dist.	S. E. Peal	2988, 3037-8, 4015-23.
1 Samaguting	Capt. J. Butler	2996.
1 Bhamo	Yunan Exped. (Anderson)	4187.
1 Yethaycoo pagoda, 2nd defile, Irrawaddy	Yunan Exped. (Anderson)	4185.
1 Moulmein	W. Theobald	3030.
1 Tenasserim	Tenasserim Exped. (Limborg)	5523.
2 Egaya, Tavoy dist.	Mus. Coll.	12662-3.
1 Pilai, Elphinstone Isle	Mergui Exped. (Anderson)	11566.
2 Kisserang	Mergui Exped. (Anderson)	11567-8.
1 Hongkong	Dr. Hungerford	11389.
1 Hongkong	Hongkong Mus. [Ex.]	12692.

(B.) MOTTLED VARIETY.

3 Andamans	Col. R. C. Tytler, A. S. B	3953, 2857-8.
2 Andamaus	V. Ball	2965, 2972.
1 Andamans	Col. B. Ford	2964.
1 Andamans	Capt. Homfray	3074.
1 Andamans	J. Wood Mason	8701.
1 Andamans	Major R. J. Wimberley	12844.
1 Tarmugli Isle, Andamans	J. Anderson	8638.

(C.) Almost uniform brown variety.

1 No loc.	No hist.	3057.

(TYPE OF T. ANDERSONI, Theobald).

1 Andamans	V. Ball	2977.
1 Cinque Isle, Andamans	Col. T. Cadell	12884.

(D.) Brown mottled variety.

5 Nicobars	F. Stoliczka	3083-7.

(TYPES OF T. MUTABILIS, Stol.).

1 Nicobars	F. A. de Roepstorf	8379.
1 Audamans	F. Stoliczka	3088.
1 No loc.	No hist.	8737.

(E.) Uniform green variety.

1 Andamans	No hist., A. S. B.	2952.
2 Andamans	Capt. Homfray	3190-1.
1 Andamans	F. Stoliczka [P.]	2960.
2 Andamans	G. E. Dobson	8520-1.
1 Andamans	F. A. de Roepstorf	2971.
1 S. Andaman	J. Wood Mason	4500.
1 Cocos Isle	Marine Survey, (Alcock)	13397.
2 Nicobars	F. A. de Roepstorf	8747, 8889.

342. TRIMERESURUS ANAMALLENSIS, Gunth.

Boulenger, p. 430.
Distribution—Hills of Southern India.

1 Cuttack	J. Wood Mason	4122.
4 Koppa, Mysore	W. M. Daly	13538-41.
1 Anamalai hills	E. Gerard [P.]	12399.
1 Anamalai hills	Col. R. H. Beddome	4400.
1 Anamalai hills	Sir J. Fayrer	3091.
3 Travancore hills	Col. R. H. Beddome	3073, 4393, 7574.
1 Travancore	Trevandrum Museum	13507.
1 Madras Pr.	J. Davison	8667.
3 No loc.	F. Stoliczka	3954, 8371-2.

343. TRIMERESURUS TRIGONOCEPHALUS, (Daud.).

Boulenger, p. 431.
Distribution—Ceylon.

1 Columbo	E. F. Kelaart, A. S. B.	3027.

344. TRIMERESURUS MACROLEPIS, Beddome.

Boulenger, p. 431.
Distribution—Hills of Southern India.

1 Anamalai hills	E. Gerard [P.]	12375.
1 Tinnevelli hills	Col. R. H. Beddome	8565.

345. TRIMERESURUS WAGLERI, Schleg.

Gunther, Reptiles Brit. Ind., p. 388.
Distribution—The Malay Peninsula and Larger Malayan Islands.

1 Singapore	R. W. G. Frith, A. S. B.	3075.

346. CRASPEDOCEPHALUS ATROX, (Linn.).

Gray, Cat. Snakes B. M., p. 6.
Distribution—Neotropical Region from Mexico to Brazil.

2 South America	E. Gerard [P.]	12401-2.

347. CRASPEDOCEPHALUS BILINEATUS, (Schleg.).

Gray, Cat. Snakes B. M., p. 7.
Distribution—South America.

1 Ecuador	E. Gerard [P.]	12391.

348. CROTALUS ADAMANTEUS, Beauv.

Garman, N. Amer. Snakes, p. 112.
Distribution—United States, N. Carolina to Texas and Mexico.

1 Alabama, U. S. A.	Dr. J. H. Garnier [Ex.]	12769.
1 San Christobal, Texas	Dr. J. H. Garnier [Ex.]	12245.
2 Texas	Dr. J. H. Garnier [Ex.]	12167, 12274.

349. CROTALUS HORRIDUS, Linn.

Garman, N. Amer. Snakes, p. 115.
Distribution—Eastern United States.

1 America	A. S. B.	3101.

350. CROTALUS MILIARIUS, Linn.

Garman, N. Amer. Snakes, p. 119.
Distribution—North America.

1 Washboro' Ont., Canada	Dr. J. H. Garnier [Ex.]	12201.

INDEX.

A.

abacurns, Hydrops, 45.
Ablabes, 18.
Acanthophis, 60.
ACROCHORDINÆ, 45.
acuminata, Dryophis, 52.
acutus, Typhlops, 3.
adamanteus, Crotalus, 74.
Adenophis, 57.
aestivus, Cyclophis, 22.
affinis, Oligodon, 25.
Ahaetulla, 35.
albocinctus, Simotes, 23.
AMBLYCEPHALIDAE, 66.
Amblycephalns, 66.
ammodytes, Vipera, 68.
anamallensis, Trimeresurus, 73.
Ancistrodon, 69.
angulatus, Uranops, 45.
annulata, Vermicella, 61.
antarcticus, Acanthophis, 60.
arenarius, Zamenis, 29.
arietans, Clotho, 68.
arnensis, Simotes, 24.
Aspidiotes, 5.
Aspidura, 12.
Atheris, 69.
atrox, Craspedocephalus, 73.
aulicus, Lycodon, 14.
aurora, Lamprophis, 13.

B.

beddomii, Tropidonotus, 37.
beddomii, Typhlops, 2.
bennetti, Hypsirhina, 55.
bernieri, Herpetodryas, 30.
berns, Pelias, 68.
bibroni, Callophis, 57.
bicolor, Pseudocyclophis, 16.
bifrenalis, Dendrophis, 35.
bilineatus, Craspedocephalus, 73.
bistrigatus, Polyodontophis, 18.
bivirgatus, Adenophis, 57.
blanfordi, Glauconia, 4.
blanfordi, Hypsirhina, 55.
blythi, Rhinophis, 7.
Blythia, 12.
Boa 5.
boddaerti, Herpetodryas, 30.
BOIDAE, 4.
Boodon, 13.
boops, Dipsas, 48.
bothriorhynchus, Typblops, 2.
bottae, Charina, 6.
brachyorrhos, Aspidura, 12.
Brachysoma, 60.
brachyura, Coronella, 20.
braminus, Typhlops, 1.
brevis, Silybura, 9.
buccata, Homalopsis, 53.
Bucephalus, 52.
bungaroides, Bungarus, 58.
Bungarus, 57.
bungarus, Naia, 59.

C.

Cacophis, 60.
caerulescens, Hydrophis, 62.
caeruleus, Bungarus, 58.
Calamaria, 10.
calamaria, Ablabes, 18.
Callophis, 56.
cana, Coronella, 20.
Cantoria, 55.
cantoris, Hydrophis, 64.
cantoris, Trimeresurus, 71.
capensis, Bncephalus, 52.
carinata, Echis, 69.
carinatus, Amblycephalus, 67.
carinatus, Herpetodryas, 30.
catenifer, Pityophis, 30.
candolineatus, Dendrelaphis, 35.
cenchoa, Dipsas, 48.
cenchria, Epicrates, 5.
cerasogaster, Xenochrophis, 45.
Cerastes, 68.
Cerberus, 54.
ceylonensis, Dipsas, 46.
ceylonicus, Bungarus, 58.
Charina, 6.
Chersydrus, 45.
chrysargus, Tropidonotus, 37.
Chrysopelea, 53.
Clotho, 68.
cobella, Liophis, 20.
Coelopeltis, 49.
collaris, Ablabes, 19.
collaris, Polyodontophis, 17.
Coluber, 31.
COLUBRIDAE, 10.
COLUBRINAE, 10.
colubrinus, Platurus, 62.
condanarus, Psammophis, 50.

conicus, Gongylophis, 5.
conspicillatus, Tropidonotus, 42.
constrictor, Boa, 5.
constrictor, Coluber, 33.
contortrix, Ancistrodon, 70.
Corallus, 5.
coronatum, Scytale, 49.
coronatus, Hydrophis, 63.
Coronella, 20.
Craspedocephalus, 73.
CROTALINAE, 69.
Crotalus, 74.
crucifer, Psammophis, 50.
cruentatus, Simotes, 24.
currori, Feylinia, 3.
curtus, Enhydris, 62.
cyanea, Dipsas, 47.
cyanocincta, Distira, 65.
Cyclophis, 21.
cyclurus, Simotes, 22.
Cylindrophis, 6.
cynodon, Dipsas, 47.

D.

dahlii, Zamenis, 29.
DASYPELTINAE, 45.
Dasypeltis, 45.
davisoni, Hydrophobus, 16.
decorata, Coronella, 20.
dekayi, Storeria, 44.
Dendrelaphis, 35.
Dendrophis, 34.
diadema, Brachysoma, 60.
diadema, Zamenis, 28.
Diadophis, 21.
diardi, Typhlops, 2.
Diemenia, 60.
dindigalensis, Silybura, 9.
dispar, Dryophis, 51.
Distira, 65.
DIPSADINAE, 45.
Dipsas, 45.
dorbignii, Heterodon, 22.
doriae, Ablabes, 18.
dorsalis, Oligodon, 25.
Dromicus, 22.
Dryophis, 51.

E.

Echis, 69.
effrene, Lycodon, 16.
Elachistodon, 48.
ELAPINAE, 56.
Elaps, 61.
elegans, Hydrophis, 64.
elegans, Psammophis, 51.
ellioti, Silybura, 9.
Enhydrina, 64.
Enhydris, 62.
enhydris, Hypsirbina, 54.
Epicrates, 5.
erythrogrammus, Hydrops, 45.
Eryx, 6.
esculapii, Coluber, 33.

F.

fasciatus, Ablabes, 20.
fasciatus, Bungarus, 57.
fasciatus, Hydrophis, 63.
fasciatus, Lycodon, 15.
fasciolatus, Zamenis, 28.
Feylinia, 3.
flagelliformis, Coluber, 33.
flaviceps, Megaerophis, 57.
Fordonia, 55.
forstenii, Dipsas, 47.
frenatus, Ablabes, 18.
fronticinctus, Dryophis, 51.
fulvius, Elaps, 61.
fusca, Dipsas, 47.
fuscum, Trachischium, 11.
fuscus, Zaoccys, 30.

G.

gammiei, Lycodon, 15.
geometricus, Boodon, 13.
Gerardia, 55.
getulus, Ophibolus, 21.
Glauconia, 4.
GLAUCONIIDAE, 4.
gokool, Dipsas, 46.
Gongylophis, 5.
Gonyophis, 34.
gouldii, Hoplocephalus, 60.
gracilis, Callophis, 57.
gracilis, Hydrophis, 64.
gracilis, Tantilla, 48.
grahamiae, Salvadora, 30.
gramineus, Trimeresurus, 72.
grandis, Silybura, 8.
granulatus, Chersydrus, 45.
guentheri, Aspidura, 12.
guentheri, Trachischium, 11.
guttatus, Coluber, 34.

H.

hardwickii, Enhydris, 62.
harrietae, Cacophis, 60.
hasselquisti, Cerastes, 68.
helena, Coluber, 31.
Helicops, 44.
Herpetodryas, 30.
Heterodon, 22.
hexagonatus, Dipsas, 47.
hexagonatus, Xenelaphis, 34.
himalayanus, Ancistrodon, 69.

himalayanus, Tropidonotus, 38.
Hipistes, 56.
hippocrepis, Zamenis, 29.
hodgsonii, Coluber, 31.
HOMALOPSINAE, 53.
Homalopsis, 53.
Homalosoma, 13.
Hoplocephalus, 60.
horridus, Crotalus, 74.
hortulanus, Corallus, 5.
Hortulia, 5.
hydrinus, Hipistes, 56.
HYDROPHIINAE, 61.
Hydrophis, 62.
Hydrophobus, 16.
Hydrops, 45.
Hydrus, 62.
hydrus, Tropidonotus, 42.
hygiae, Elaps, 61.
hypnale, Ancistrodon, 70.
Hypsirhina, 54.

I.

ILYSIIDAE, 6.
intestinalis, Adenophis, 57.
irregularis, Ahaetulla, 36.

J.

jaculus, Eryx, 6.
jara, Lycodon, 14.
jerdoni, Distira, 65.
jerdoni, Trimeresurus, 71.
jerdoni, Typhlops, 2.
johnii, Eryx, 6.

K.

karelini, Zamenis, 28.
korros, Zamenis, 26.

L.

lacertina, Coelopeltis, 49.
ladaccensis, Zamenis, 27.
Lamprophis, 13.
lapemidoides, Distira, 66.
laticaudatus, Platurus, 61.
latifasciatus, Hydrophis, 63.
leberis, Tropidonotus, 44.
lebetina, Vipera, 68.
lecontei, Rhinochoilus, 21.
leithii, Psammophis, 50.
lemniscatus, Elaps, 61.
Leptodeira, 48.
Leptognathus, 67.
leucobalia, Fordonia, 55.
leucomelas, Tropidonotus, 42.
lineata, Typhlina, 3.
lineatus, Boodon, 13.
lineatus, Dromicus, 22.
lineolatum, Taphrometopum, 49.
liocercus, Ahaetulla, 36.
Liophis, 20.
lividus, Bungarus, 58.
lutrix, Homalosoma, 13.
Lycodon, 13.

M.

maclellandi, Callophis, 56.
macrolepis Trimeresurus, 73.
macrops, Pseudoxenodon, 36
macularius, Amblycephalus, 67.
maculata, Silybura, 8.
maculatus, Cylindrophis, 7.
maculiceps, Callophis, 56.
madurensis, Platyplectrurus, 10.
margaritatus, Gonyophis, 34.
Megaerophis, 57.
melanocephalus, Aspidiotes, 5.
melanocephalus, Oligodon, 26.
melanocephalus, Polyodontophis, 18.
melanogaster, Silybura, 7.
melanoleucus, Pityophis, 30.
melanurus, Coluber, 32.
merremii, Liophis, 21.
miliarius, Crotalus, 74.
modestus, Ablabes, 19.
modestus, Amblycephalus, 66.
modestus, Tropidonotus, 36.
moellendorffii, Amblycephalus, 67.
molurus, Python, 4.
monticola, Amblycephalus, 66.
monticola, Trachischium, 12.
monticola, Trimeresurus, 70.
monticola, Tropidonotus, 39.
Morelia, 4.
mucosus, Zamenis, 26.
multifasciatus, Dipsas, 46.
multimaculata, Dipsas, 46.
mycterizans, Dryophis, 52.

N.

Naia, 59.
natrix, Tropidonotus, 43.
natteri, Thamnodynastes, 48.
nebulatus, Leptognathus, 67.
nicobarensis, Tropidonotus, 42.
nicobariensis, Ablabes, 19.
nigra, Silybura, 8.
nigrescens, Callophis, 56.
nigrescens, Typhlops, 3.
nigrocinctus, Elaps, 61.
nigrocinctus, Hydrophis, 63.
nigrocinctus, Tropidonotus, 37.
nigromarginatus, Zaoccys, 29.
nitida, Silybura, 8.
nympha, Hydrophobus, 16.

O.

obscurus, Hydrophis, 63.
obsoletus, Coluber 33.
occipitomaculata, Storeria, 44.
ocellata, Silybura, 8.
octolineatus, Simotes, 24.
Oligodon, 25.
olivacea, Diemenia, 60.
Ophibolus, 21.
ornata, Chrysopelea, 53.
oxycephalus, Coluber, 33.
oxyrhynchus, Rhinophis, 7.

P.

pallasii, Ancistrodon, 70.
parallelus, Tropidonotus, 37.
pavimentata, Calamaria, 10.
pealii, Tropidonotus, 41,
Pelias, 68.
perroteti, Dryophis, 51.
perroteti, Plectrurus, 9.
perroteti, Xylophis, 11.
persicus, Cerastes, 68.
persicus, Pseudocyclophis, 17.
persicus, Typhlops, 3.
petersii, Silybura, 8.
phocarum, Coronella, 20.
pictus, Dendrophis, 34.
pictus, Psammodynastes, 49.
piscator, Tropidonotus, 40.
Pityophis, 30.
planiceps, Simotes, 25.
Platurus, 61.
platurus, Hydrus, 62.
platyceps, Tropidonotus, 36.
Platyplectrurus, 10.
platyrhinus, Heterodon, 22.
Plectrurus, 9.
plumbea, Hypsirhina, 54.
plumbicolor, Tropidonotus, 41.
Polyodontophis, 17.
porphyraceus, Ablabes, 19.
porphyriacus, Pseudechis, 60.
porrectus, Typhlops, 2.
prasinus, Coluber, 32.
prasinus, Dryophis, 51.
prevostiana, Gerardia, 55.
producta, Rhagerrhis, 26.
Psammodynastes, 49.
Psammophis, 50.
Psammophylax, 26.
Pseudechis, 60.
Pseudocyclophis, 16.
Pseudoxenodon, 36.
pulneyensis, Silybura, 7.
pulverulentus, Dryophis, 52.
pulverulentus, Psammodynastes, 49.
punctatus, Diadophis, 21.
punctulata, Dendrophis, 35.
punctulatus, Tropidonotus, 41.
purpurascens, Simotes, 23.
purpureomaculatus, Trimeresurus, 71.
Python, 4.

R.

radiatus, Coluber, 32.
rappii, Ablabes, 19.
ravergieri, Zamenis, 29.
regia, Hortulia, 5.
reginae, Liophis, 21.
reticularis, Coluber, 31.
reticulata, Blythia, 12.
reticulata, Diemenia, 60.
reticulatus, Python, 4.
rhabdocephalus, Xenodon, 36.
Rhagerrhis, 26.
Rhinocheilus, 21.
Rhinophis, 7.
rhinopoma, Dipsas, 48.
rhodomelas, Tropidonotus, 42.
rhombeatus, Psammophylax, 26.
rhynchops, Cerberus, 54
robusta, Distira, 65.
rubescens, Chrysopelea, 53.
rubrolineata, Silybura, 9.
rubromaculata, Silybura, 9.
rufescens, Leptodeira, 48.
rufus, Cylindrophis, 6.
russellii, Vipera, 67.

S.

sagittarius, Polyodontophis, 17.
Salvadora, 30.
sanguineus, Platyplectrurus, 10.
sanguineus, Rhinophis, 7.
saurita, Tropidonotus, 43.
scabra, Dasypeltis, 45.
schistosus, Helicops, 44.
scriptus, Ablabes, 18.
Scytale, 49.
semifasciatus, Bungarus, 58.
sibilans, Psammophis, 50.
sieboldii, Hypsirhina, 55.
signatus, Simotes, 25.
Silybura, 7.
Simotes, 22.
sipedon, Tropidonotus, 44.
sirtalis, Tropidonotus, 43.
smaragdina, Ahaetulla, 35.
spilotes, Morelia, 4.
squamata, Atheris, 69.
stahlknechti, Calamaria, 11.
stolatus, Tropidonotus, 39.
stoliczkae, Ablabes, 18.
Storeria, 44.
striatula, Virginia, 13.

striatus, Lycodon, 13.
strigatus, Trimeresurus, 70.
subannulatus, Hydrophobus, 16.
subcinctus, Lycodon, 16.
subgriseus, Oligodon, 25.
sublineatus, Oligodon, 25.
subminiatus Tropidonotus, 38.
subocularis Dendrophis, 35.
subpunctatus, Polyodontophis, 17.
subradiatus Coluber, 33.
sumatrana, Calamaria, 11.
syriacus, Typhlops, 3.

T.

taeniatus, Coluber, 33.
taeniurus, Coluber, 31.
Tantilla, 48.
Taphrometopum, 49.
tenasserimensis, Zaoccys, 30.
tenuiceps, Trachischium, 11.
Thamuodynastes, 48.
thebaicus, Eryx, 6.
theobaldi, Simotes, 24.
theobaldianus, Typhlops, 3.
tigrinus, Tropidonotus, 43.
Trachischium, 11.
trachyprocta, Aspidura, 12.
travancoricus, Lyoodon, 14.
trevelyanus, Rhinophis, 7.
trianguligerus, Ophibolus, 21.
trianguligerus, Tropidonotus, 42.
tricolor, Ablabes, 20.
trigonata, Dipsas, 45.
trigonocephalus, Trimeresurus, 73.
trilineatus, Platyplectrurus. 10.
trimaculatus, Callophis, 56.
Trimeresurus, 70.
tripudians, Naia, 59.
Tropidonotus, 36.
tuberculata, Distira, 65.
Typhlina, 3.
TYPHLOPIDAE, 1.
Typhlops, 1.

U.

unicolor, Boodon, 13.
unicolor, Xenopeltis, 10.
Uranops, 45.
UROPELTIDAE, 7.

V.

valakadien, Enhydrina, 64.
variegata, Morelia, 4.
ventrimaculatus, Zamenis, 27.
Vermicella, 61.
vernalis, Cyclophis, 21.
vibakari, Tropidonotus, 41.
violacea, Cantoria, 55.
violaceus, Simotes, 23.
Vipera, 67.
VIPERIDAE, 67.
viperina, Distira, 66.
VIPERINAE, 67.
Virginia, 18.
vittatus, Tropidonotus 43,

W.

wagleri, Trimeresurus, 73.
westermanni, Elachistodon, 48.
woodmasoni, Simotes, 24.

X.

Xenelaphis, 34.
Xenochrophis, 45.
Xenodon, 36.
XENOPELTIDAE, 10.
Xenopeltis. 10.
Xylophis, 11.

Z.

Zamenis, 26.
Zaoccys, 29.